Edge of Daylight

by

Eddie Askew

By the same author:
A Silence and A Shouting
Disguises of Love
Many Voices One Voice
No Strange Land
Facing the Storm
Breaking the Rules
Cross Purposes
Slower than Butterflies
Music on the Wind

Published by
The Leprosy Mission International
80 Windmill Road
Brentford
Middlesex TW8 0QH, United Kingdom

First published in 2000

Paintings and drawings by the author

Editorial and Design by Craft Plus Publishing Ltd
53 Crown Street, Brentwood, Essex CM14 4NN

Printed in Spain
A catalogue record for this book is available from the British Library

ISBN 0 902731 42 4 Hard back edition
ISBN 0 902731 43 2 Soft back edition

With thanks to Andrew Motion for his permission to quote
from his poem *Mythology*.

Cover picture: Part of Morning mist, Nepal, Watercolour, 1998

Dedication

To my family
Barbara
Jenny and Peter
Sam and Jessamy
Stephanie and Howard
Claudia and Georgia

'Earth's axle creaks; the year jolts on; the trees
begin to slip their brittle leaves, their flakes of rust;
and darkness takes the edge of daylight, not
because it wants to – never that. Because it must.'

Andrew Motion

Purulia landscape
Watercolour sketch
1998

Foreword

Being the daughters of the infamous Eddie Askew, we felt we wanted to write the foreword of this book, as we were part of it. It is, in a way, as much our story as it is his, although we were in the background, happily growing up in the warm Indian sunshine, very much protected from what we now know as the real world.

Along with Dad's career with The Leprosy Mission, from an early age we were aware of his creative talent (as well as his sense of humour!), beginning with his first exhibition of paintings in a dark church hall in Darjeeling. Now we are thrilled and so proud of how his life has developed – his books, his paintings, the retreats and quiet days, and now this – his story.

We continue to watch in awe, wondering where life will take him next. Dad, we love you.

Enjoy the book, feel the warmth of India and her people, celebrate the achievements of The Leprosy Mission, and laugh with us as you get a glimpse of how it was.

Read on.

With love,

Jenny and Stephanie

All the paintings and sketches in the book are by Eddie Askew.
While the words are his memoirs, the paintings are roughly in
chronological order, so also showing his developing art.

Introduction

For some time I've resisted strongly suggestions that I should write my memoirs. I've yawned my way through too many pages of them. Pages put together by worthy people who've insisted on sharing their stories with the public, whether the public wanted them or not. So why should I inflict mine on anyone? The comment that changed things came from Jenny, one of our two daughters. She said, 'When you die someone will write a lot of sentimental twaddle about you and they'll probably get it all wrong. Much better write it yourself and get it right.' In other words 'Get your version in first'. So here it is.

I don't claim that my version is any more accurate than anyone else's would be. Memory is selective and often creative. It easily deceives. It can put a personal gloss on achievements that belong collectively to a group of people rather than an individual. What seems true to me may not seem that way to colleagues who view it from a different perspective. Ego puts itself in the centre of the picture and claims more credit than it deserves. I'm conscious of this even though I may not always recognise the danger when it happens. Some of the experiences I've described have been fleeting, and events which have been one-off adventures for me have been ordinary daily living for others. But I've tried to be honest and have been helped by tour diaries, reports and circular letters kept over the years.

There are many people I should thank. Barbara first, the companion who has been with me throughout and who has made much of this possible by her unfailing love and support. Also our daughters Stephanie and Jennifer, who mean more to us as the years go by. Special thanks to two Chairmen of The Leprosy Mission International, Sir Eric Richardson and the late Rev. Dr. Ronald Goulding. Both offered wisdom, strength and support during my time in the International Office of the Mission. Audrey Pyle too deserves deep appreciation for her work as my Personal Assistant over many years and as a good and reliable friend. Also thanks to the Poet Laureate, Andrew Motion, for kind permission to quote from his poetry. And finally a thank you to all my colleagues, women and men who have worked selflessly, enthusiastically and usually gladly over the years to help those who suffer in many countries. God bless you all.

Eddie Askew

CONTENTS

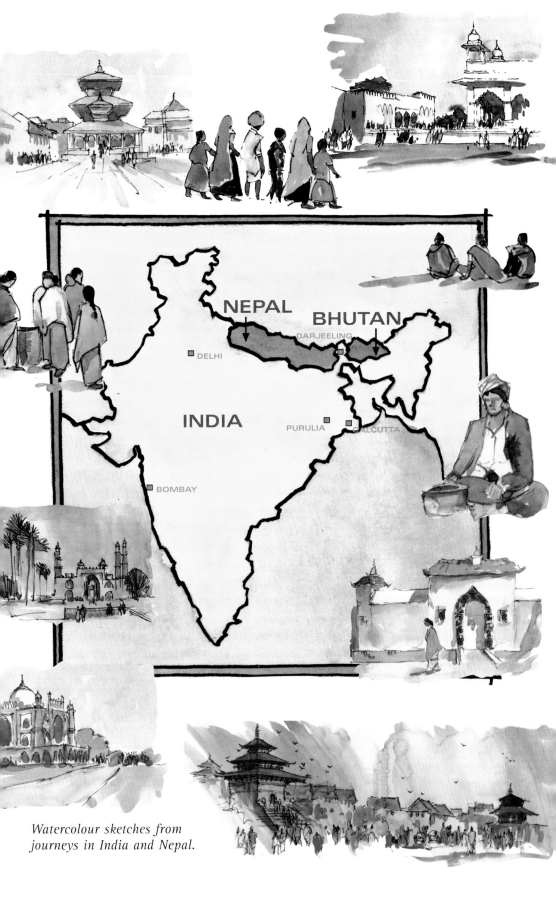

NEPAL

BHUTAN

DARJEELING

DELHI

INDIA

PURULIA

CALCUTTA

BOMBAY

Watercolour sketches from journeys in India and Nepal.

CHAPTER ONE

In at the Deep End

It was the quiet that woke us. The ship's engines had stopped. There was no movement. Bright sunshine poured honey into the cabin through the open porthole. Raucous black crows screeched as they fought the acrobatic and aggressive seagulls for food. A morality play in black and white. With the sun and the

Indian Village

noise came the smell, unfamiliar, acrid. It was a mixture of salt sea, diesel oil and the damp aroma of rotting vegetation.

We looked out onto the dock. It was a jumble of hawsers and piles of crates. Seemingly disorganised groups of shouting coolies walked through the litter of broken coconut shells. Our first glimpse of Bombay. It was the excitement of new experience. The heat, the colour and the noise were so different from the drabness and rationing of post-war Britain. In India the rationing was caused by poverty although we didn't realise that yet.

Barbara and I were married in October 1950 and sailed for India a month later. There were family doubts from both sides and some opposition. "You won't get a bloody medal you know," said one irate parent. It was hard to explain. India seemed a long way from home. To go there for five years to work amongst leprosy patients didn't seem the sanest thing a young couple could do.

Two weeks' sailing. Bay of Biscay, Mediterranean, a shopping trip at Port Said and through the Suez Canal. Another stop at Aden and then Bombay. Almost no one went by air then. Communication was slow. Telephones hardly worked over those distances. Letters took five or six days each way if you were lucky and if no unscrupulous philatelist en route steamed the stamps off the envelope. It was tough for the families at home, less so for us. We saw it as part Christian commitment, part adventure. It's hard to know which part predominated then.

We must have looked ridiculous as we walked through Bombay wearing our large solar topis against the tropical sun. We'd bought them in Port Said on the Suez Canal, on the advice of an experienced senior missionary. She was still living in the 1930s although we didn't know it at the time. After the first few days, and observing how few people seemed to wear them, we put them away and only brought them out for party games at Christmas. Our learning had begun, although we still had to realise how silly a man looked in khaki shorts which almost covered his knees.

Two full nights and a day followed on the Howrah Express, an optimistic name. It was a rattling, dusty, smoky train. It occasionally reached 30 miles an hour all out but not for long. It took us a thousand miles across India to Purulia in what is now part of West Bengal. Purulia was a small crowded district town, a jumble of houses and shops along a twisting main street just wide enough for two bullock carts to scrape past each other. The street was unpaved, its edges defined by open drains, their aroma always noticeable but strongest in the hot weather when their contents decayed quickest. The road was always busy with people, *pi* dogs and wandering cows. The dogs and cows enlivened the grounds of the government offices and law courts set within an expanse of rice fields. It was an untidy but vibrant place.

We stood on the platform surrounded by luggage. There was no one to meet us. The telegram hadn't arrived on time. Telegrams rarely did. They usually came two days after the confirmatory letter. I found the stationmaster and asked if he'd phone the Leprosy Hospital. He looked blank. Hospitals in rural India didn't have telephones, particularly leprosy hospitals.

Eventually we were spotted by a hospital worker who was at the railway station on other business. He was a tiny man hardly in control of a large bicycle. His feet only touched the pedals during the top half of their rotation and the leather saddle was shiny from the resultant friction. He organised us into two ramshackle horse-drawn coaches straight out of a Western film set. The small, long-suffering horses were old and decrepit, their ribs showing clear. So were the drivers although their ribs were covered by torn shirts. We'd arrived. Four naive English folk – Max Hopwood, very tall, rather clumsy, and recently qualified as a doctor, Marian Rees, an experienced nurse, my wife Barbara, an expert secretary with Red Cross experience and me, a qualified but green school teacher.

Purulia Leprosy Home and Hospital was the largest leprosy centre in India. About 800 long-stay patients lived there, including 120 child patients. The Leprosy Mission had always financed the centre but the senior staff had been provided by the Church Missionary Society until now. They had worked through the difficult years of austerity during World War Two and were exhausted. The Leprosy Mission had to find its own staff. A doctor, nurse and schoolteacher were needed urgently.

Within weeks, without any advertising or publicity, we had each offered ourselves for service. Barbara and I were invited to meet Dr Neil Fraser, home on leave after years in China. More recently he'd set up the Mission's new leprosy centre in Hong Kong – Hay Ling Chau, the Isle of Happy Healing. He interviewed us in his home in Shrewsbury. The meeting seemed to go well, although he told us years later that his very elderly father had suspected me of stealing the teaspoons. I didn't need to. We'd got four sets among our wedding presents.

Twenty four years on, when I was appointed the Mission's International Director, I asked if my personal files were still in the archives. They were. I asked to see them. Neil Fraser's report of that first interview was recorded. He recommended us for service although he said he felt that "Barbara is more mature than Eddie but I can see possibilities in him." Not an exact quote but it'll do. I don't know what he saw but he said while I was well qualified as a teacher he saw my future in administration and as a possible leader. I've always been grateful for those who could see possibilities in other people and have tried to do the same.

Within a month of arriving in Purulia I was desperately ill with typhoid. I'd had all the recommended inoculations but they didn't seem to help. We were living in a small house without electricity, with no running water. There was no proper bathroom and only an outside bore hole latrine, Indian style. My memory of the time is patchy. My bed was too short and my legs stuck out uncomfortably over the end. Barbara remedied this with my drawing board and a cushion. There were dramatic night sweats, high temperatures and headaches. It was an anxious time for Barbara, married two months. Less so for me, I was hardly conscious of what might happen.

On the way towards recovery Christmas Day brought me a slice of toast, an enema and a small undistinguished puppy. His legs trembled about as weakly as mine and we named him Chivers, after the jelly. From then on things could only get better.

They did. We immersed ourselves in the local language, Bengali. A different script of 57 signs and many joint letters including 11 vowels, but at least it was phonetic. Once you could hear the sounds correctly – as correctly as a Western European could – you could spell accurately. Some of the early exercises were hilarious. *Panch kaak kakar kane bashe achhe – five crows are perched on my uncle's ear.* I found a very old English to Bengali phrase book written for travellers. *Saddle the elephant for early dawn tomorrow* it translated. I tried it out on the man who worked in our small garden. It confirmed his opinion of Europeans. Next day there was no elephant and the gardener looked suspiciously at me every time I tried to speak to him.

His name inappropriately was Gabriel, but he was more a Bengali leprechaun than an archangel. Our breakfasts were sent over from the Superintendent's bungalow across the road and Gabriel kept our boiled eggs warm on the journey in the breast pocket of his grubby shirt. Fortunately, the shells were still intact.

There were daily language lessons. First with Lavinia Bose, a tiny, gorgeous dumpling of a Bengali lady, cultured and courteous but firm. She was keen on getting our pronunciation right, perhaps especially because of her blindness, and because the dialect of the Purulia area was less than pure Bengali. Later we moved on to Sachendra Choudhury, a local schoolmaster, who concentrated on our grammar and writing.

After four months we packed our bags and books and made another three-day journey north by rail and ferry over the River Ganges. We went to Darjeeling for three months' intensive study at language school. We joined about 30 students of one sort or another, all missionaries and of several nationalities. The single ones lived in the school but we rented a wooden cottage 7,000 feet above sea level with breathtaking views of the Himalayas. Range after range of sculpted mountain ridges, often rising from a sea of morning mist to the heights of Kanchenjunga, 28,000 feet high. The early mornings could be magical and I would be up at dawn ready to paint. Often the hillside was shrouded in mist but as the sun came up the clouds would burn away and the snows of the high Himalayas would stand in glory. A challenge for my watercolours.

Darjeeling was a fascinating hill town; a mixture of Nepali, Lepcha and Sherpa people. There were Tibetans as well. Tall tough men with long plaits of black hair hanging down their backs. Women too, wind tanned and wearing chunky necklaces of silver, amber and turquoise. It was and still is a centre for the tea industry. The pioneers of the British Raj knew how to choose sites for hill stations. Chowrasta, the highest road of the town is a promenade of shops and small cafés. From there narrow streets twist down hill through a jumble of red and green painted corrugated roofs. Untidy lines of wooden buildings descend to the vegetable market and butchers' stalls, past noisy foursomes at the roadside playing energetic card games or carom. The air is clear and cool. It catches your throat as you labour for breath before acclimatising to the altitude. It was a fascinating mix of cultures but with few Bengalis in those days it wasn't a great place for developing conversational skills in the language.

We went back to Purulia with a little more confidence. We needed an outlet for what we had learned and were still learning. Barbara and I began to teach in the school for children with leprosy. Still limited in what we could say and understand we began with practical classes with older children. Barbara taught sewing and embroidery to both boys and girls. Coming from remote villages many of them had never seen a needle used, except by occasional itinerant male tailors who travelled the countryside with their portable sewing machines and set up in a village for a few days to make clothes and then move on.

I was to take over the school from Mary Macdonald who was ready to go on home leave and wasn't planning to return. Mary was an uncompromising take-no-prisoners evangelical. She was determined and it was hard to disagree with her. Her prayers could have left no doubt in God's mind about what she expected him to do. She did a first class job organising the school from scratch. She inspired the teachers but her aggressive approach didn't do much for me. I preferred then, as I do now, to tackle problems in a way that doesn't avoid disagreement but which leaves open the possibility of reaching an understanding with those who think differently.

There were moments of drama which turned to comedy. Barbara was annoyed by the misbehaviour of a 15-year-old boy. She summoned all the Bengali at her command and began to tell him off. Halfway through and very politely he held up his hand to interrupt. "You made a mistake there," he said. "You should have said it this way," and continued to tell himself off.

My group of teenagers did some bookbinding, a bit of art, but mostly odd jobs around the compound. Not as cheap labour but as part of their introduction to work. We learned some elementary bricklaying, gardening and general repairs. We chipped rust off old but serviceable steel joists and repainted them. It wasn't the only thing they repainted. In my absence a black goat made the mistake of getting within brush distance. By the time I returned it was on the way to becoming a frantic brown and very sticky goat. Today it could have been entered for the Turner Prize.

One day in the art class I sent the boys out to wander through the hospital grounds and bring back something they thought beautiful. Several brought flowers, one a multicoloured stone, another a leaf. One brought a small cauliflower. "Why do you think that's beautiful?" I asked. "Because you can eat it," he replied. Food is beautiful in a breadline economy where two meals a day is luxury.

The local teachers were a lovely crowd, all patients or ex-patients themselves and with a tremendous sympathy for the children in their care. A few stand out. There was Rajen. His father and elder brother had come to the centre first. When father saw the place was good he sent for his wife and younger son. The son was Rajen. All the family had leprosy, unusual but not unknown. During the years of treatment they became Christians. The father's leprosy ran its course through whatever treatment was available then. One foot was amputated and he lost several fingers. His village refused to have him back. He built a small house near the hospital but was burgled three times. He could have had little to take but others had less and he finished with nothing. The Mission took him back and gave him shelter. As a young man Rajen became a teacher in the hospital school and, with the coming of the drug dapsone, he was healed without any disability. He was helped to find a home outside the centre and joined the staff as a teacher.

Cornelius was a sensitive, thoughtful and very intelligent Christian man in his late twenties. He'd been in the hospital since childhood, left there by parents who then disappeared. He too was cured and, in spite of having no formal qualifications, we managed to get him into a Government Teacher Training College. He took one of the top places in the final exams and came back to give a life-time's service to the hospital. He married happily and became a respected elder in his community.

Dharmamay was emotional, easily moved, his own life severely affected by leprosy. He had seriously disabled hands and a stammer, but a glowing faith.

Pramodh had come late and reluctantly to the hospital. He had a university degree, spoke fluent English and had been a teacher already. He came to us angry and cynical, the effect of the ostracism he'd faced. But he taught well and as time passed took an increasingly positive role in the community. I learned a lot from Pramodh, particularly when he questioned some of what he saw as our unconscious colonial attitudes.

The classrooms were scattered around the compound. Some classes had to use rooms in the children's boarding houses, others in tumble-down buildings always needing repairs. In our first two years we were able to build a new well-designed school with grants from the Mission. Semi-detached classrooms, light and airy, formed a semicircle facing an assembly hall, a craft centre, teachers' rooms and stores. The garden, fenced off from hungry, marauding goats and wandering cattle, blossomed gloriously in the cooler season. Great incandescent splashes of extrovert scarlet, yellows and purples from hibiscus, cannas and zinnias. In the hot weather there was the heady fragrance of frangipani, tulip trees, the lovely blue of jacaranda and the bright vermilion of *palash*, the flame of the forest.

Children and teachers accepted the new school with great enthusiasm. We had hardly moved in when disaster struck. Weather plays unpredictable tricks as the seasons change. The cooler weather was drawing to a close. The sun was becoming less friendly and flexing its muscles in earnest. Then the storm came. Heavy clouds gathered on the horizon. The sky darkened until it was blacker than we'd ever seen. By late afternoon we were walking in twilight. The wind whipped up a dust storm, choking and threatening. The evening was punctuated with thunder, first distant then overhead. Brilliant stabs of lightning were followed almost immediately by great vicious cracks of sound. We shuttered the windows and barred the doors. We went to bed apprehensive but expecting no more than the usual small damage storms caused. An odd tree branch snapped, a bit of fencing broken.

We woke very early to a howling cyclone. Rain sheeting almost horizontally, lit by tremendous flashes of lightning, trees crashing down in the dark. The fury was awe-inspiring. The storm lasted about an hour although over the next 48 hours more than 12 inches of rain fell. The worst over, we tried to drive up to the hospital in the early morning. Over 100 trees were down, some of them giants. They lay across the roads, their roots contorted in protest at the way they'd been torn from the ground. The holes left by the violence were full of water. Some trees had fallen across patients' houses but although they were damaged their concrete roofs had stood up to the impact. Except for one building. An enormous *pipal* tree had fallen across one ward and the roof of one room had crashed down. Tons of concrete over their beds. Against all expectations the patients living there were alive and well. Minutes before they'd got up and walked out onto the veranda to watch the drama around them.

Then we saw the wreckage of the school. The roofs of almost every building were shattered. The lovely semi-circular clay pantiles covered the ground like unseasonal autumn leaves, the wooden battens of the roofs bare and skeletal against the sky. The rooms were flooded, books, papers and equipment soaked. We were devastated. After all the planning, hard work and expense our hopes were gone. We rallied. One thing we had in plenty was labour. Many of our patients in those days were fit for work. They were in hospital more through the fear and prejudice of their communities than through serious disability – although we had the disabled too – and we quickly organised a re-roofing programme. In a few weeks the school was repaired and back in action again.

The healthy children were a smaller group of about 60. They were children whose parents had leprosy but who had developed no signs of the illness themselves. Medical opinion then strongly favoured segregation for health reasons so they lived separately from their parents who were under treatment and who were encouraged to visit them and stay in touch. Some did, others didn't. Today with greater knowledge and more effective medicines the children would continue to live at home with their families while their parents were under treatment. We ran a small school for the healthy children but only at primary level. Later they faced a great deal of prejudice as we tried to get them admitted into higher classes in local government schools. Their background and connection with a leprosy hospital was enough to make ordinary schools reject them.

To combat this problem we eventually reached an agreement with two Christian boarding schools in another part of Bengal to take them on when they passed the level we could deal with. School certificates from these schools were acceptable where Purulia Leprosy Home School certificates were not.

Rupen was a great character. He had a tragic family background with a mother who was a severely disabled patient. He progressed from our small school to one of the boarding schools. He was bright, effervescent and a great favourite, but couldn't pass the Indian equivalent of his O levels. He failed them twice.

The government charged fees for the exams and I said we couldn't pay a third time. He asked if I would let him sit them again if he found the money. I agreed although I had no idea where he'd get the money from. He found it, re-sat the exams and passed. I thought better of ever asking him where the money had come from.

We arranged for him to take a six-month course of training as a physiotherapy technician. This would give him enough background to work in a leprosy centre doing basic routines. He so impressed his tutor that she recommended him for a full three-year physiotherapy training course. Today he is happily married with teenage children of his own and is the senior physio in a hospital in a large Indian industrial town.

Black rocks, Ragunathpur
Watercolour
1951

CHAPTER TWO

Beginnings

Eddie aged seven

My father was killed on April Fool's Day 1945.
I was not quite eighteen. He was serving in the
Royal Navy on one of its newest and most
powerful aircraft carriers, *HMS Indefatigable*.
It was part of the Pacific Fleet.

On 1st April they were supporting the American landings on Okinawa against
fierce resistance when the fleet was attacked by Japanese *kamikaze* suicide
planes. The pilots simply aimed their aircraft at the target and crashed into it
with their bombs. One got through the gunfire and exploded on the *Indefatigable*.

Years later one of my father's shipmates wrote to me. '...*I was alongside your
father when the Japanese kamikaze plane came screaming out of the sky. We
were both ammunition loaders for B gun and we all stayed at our post to the
very last second. I managed to duck behind something (memory a bit vague
there). There was such a big flash and your father died instantly, such a brave
man... Your father was a kind, caring man, a little religious – I remember well he
used to say his prayers every night, and never swore like most sailors did and he
did his duty loyally.*'

The story is also recorded in *Sakishima and Back*, a book by Stuart Eldon,
who was an RNVR Lieutenant on the ship. He quotes one of the stewards,
Norman Grey: '...*Askew, who kneeled to say his prayers every night, had been up
near the bridge. Only his glasses were found... (after the explosion)... The thought
of Askew praying, despite their scorn, which they now regretted, made some
begin to think about their own beliefs. I spent a few hours down in the chapel.*'

Other witnesses had slightly different memories. I suppose there isn't a good
day to be killed but April Fool's Day seemed to be worse than most. I was at
school the day the telegram arrived. That was some time later of course, news
travelled slowly in those days. I got home to find mother prostrate with grief. I
read the telegram. It was only later that I realised that April Fool's Day 1945 was
also Easter Sunday, the day of resurrection. That was a belated comfort.

Dad had been a skilled factory worker in the hosiery industry, making ladies' silk
stockings. He was a quiet, retiring man, gentle but firm in his beliefs. He was
teetotal. He and mother were committed members of the Salvation Army and he
was secretary of the local corps until he joined the Royal Navy when my mother
took on the responsibility.

She was the more openly determined character of the two. In some ways
ahead of her time, she never smacked me, but when I offended her, her silences
could last a couple of days. Smacking would have been a lesser sentence. She
had a sense of fun although this was sometimes overlaid by the worry of keeping
a family fed and clothed during the recessions of the 1930s. Father was never
out of work but frequently on what was called 'short time' – three days work a
week and paid accordingly. We never went hungry but there were few luxuries.

As an only child in Nottingham my life was carefree. With friends I played and quarrelled in the woods a mile or more from home. Caught sticklebacks in the stream and brought back freshwater crayfish to keep alive in water-filled biscuit tins. My bedroom cupboard was crammed with books – all the children's classics together with *Beano* and *Dandy* annuals. I can't remember a time when I didn't read, and my eventual introduction to the local children's library was the nearest thing to heaven I knew. Later, as an early and self-conscious teenager I began working my way through the classics, mostly bought for a few coppers from a large second-hand book shop in town. I worked through Dickens, H.G.Wells, Homer's *Iliad* and *Odyssey* and the Romantic poets. There was much I didn't understand but I think it gave me an appreciation of good writing that stayed with me.

I remember my first day at the local Church of England Primary School when I was five. I was very proud of the fact that I was the only boy who didn't cry when his mother left him to the teachers' mercy. I also remember sitting at my first desk and being given a small blackboard and a box of coloured chalks to draw with. I suppose I must have drawn pictures at home before that but this was the beginning of my odyssey as an artist.

I was consistently top of the class with Sid, my friend and rival, always second. He was tough, occasionally a bully. One day we fought in the playground. The headmaster caught us and we were caned. Discipline was direct and unquestioned in those days. We were both encouraged by this same headmaster and our class teacher, and we both won free grammar school places. But then our paths divided. Because his family couldn't meet the extra expenses he missed the chance of a better education. This was, I think, my first political experience. My mother went out to work to meet the costs for me. She took the first job she could find, as cleaner in a local furniture store. Years later she had worked her way up to become head cashier in one of Nottingham's largest department stores in spite of her lack of any formal qualifications.

Life was quiet. Milk was delivered by horse and trap and measured out into jugs on the doorstep. It was the back door for traders, the front door only for special guests. We ran out into the garden if we heard an aeroplane. That changed though in the early 1940s. Hurricanes and Spitfires flew from a nearby airfield and I remember vividly standing out in the summer dusk on several nights watching hundreds of four-engined Lancaster bombers circling above us at different altitudes. They rendezvoused to begin the thousand bomber raids on German cities like Dresden in retaliation for German bombing of Coventry and other places. After the war a group of German students came over to Coventry to help with the rebuilding of the cathedral. I once told the story to our Indian bishop, Dilbar Hans, a charismatic personality and the first national bishop for the diocese. "And did any of your young men go over to Germany to help rebuild Dresden?" he asked gently.

Family hopes for me almost came to grief. At 13 a short series of headaches led to surgery, a mastoidectomy behind my right ear. Infection set in. Meningitis. I was in a coma for several days. Penicillin was still in the future and my parents were warned that I probably wouldn't live. I did, but spent 18 weeks in hospital during the evacuation of the British Army from France through Dunkirk, although I don't think it would have made any difference to the war if I'd not been in hospital. As I recovered strength during these weeks I had little to do. I began to draw again, first copying Disney cartoons, then moving on to making up my own pictures. The nurses were impressed and from then on drawing and painting became an integral, if spasmodic, part of my life.

When Dad was killed Mother withdrew into her own private world of grief. It lasted several years through much of my own time in the Navy until she re-met and married an old family friend. It was a happy relationship that lasted until her death at 84.

The Salvation Army must have laid a basis of Christian knowledge and attitude but as I entered my teens it wasn't my scene. Reluctance grew. Teaching at the grammar school was science orientated, encouraging us to question, analyse and look for proof. Heady stuff for a teenager. I took a firm stance as an agnostic, refusing to take part in school prayers. It was just good old-fashioned teenage rebellion, although it wasn't called that in those days. In fact the word teenager hadn't yet arrived from the United States. If it had I'd probably have conformed, as a rebellion against identified rebellion, if you see what I mean.

Through all the questioning I still said my routine prayers at night. It was part habit, part comfort blanket, and perhaps part insurance policy in case God did exist after all. Then at 17 and still in the sixth form I was attracted to a youth group at a Baptist church. It wasn't the worship, the theology or the evangelism that attracted me, it was the number of girls of my own age. Conversion by hormones. I joined the group and was accepted without question. Meetings included a mixture of raucous and sometimes very physical games. Country dancing was macho style but there were also gentle invitations to Sunday evening worship.

I went, sitting in the gallery with just a few friends. I usually played chess during the sermon with a portable set I carried around. But the services were different. The minister, Reg Baker, a tall, thin man full of a natural dignity when he wasn't fooling around with the gang, was down to earth and very positive. Life was to be lived fully, even in the war years. Christian faith was about growth and developing one's individuality, not about negative restrictions. Far more do's than don'ts. I saw that Christians could laugh and play practical jokes. Going to the loo in his house was an adventure. Open the door and you were likely to find a life-size bust of Beethoven dressed in an academic gown sitting there.

During the last years of the war he and other leaders took us on walking holidays in North Wales. I remember him doing a Punch and Judy act from the open window of the railway carriage door each time the train pulled into any station. It astounded the would-be passengers – and also kept our compartment free of intruders. I responded to his lifestyle and asked for baptism.

I met Barbara here. I saw an attractive, dark-haired and brown-eyed extrovert, always surrounded by friends, mostly male. I joined them. She was effervescent and warm. I asked her out. Our first date was to The Little Theatre, the local repertory theatre with Madame Blanche Laughton and her Bijou Orchestra, four people altogether. Very bijou. The play was *Dr. Jekyll and Mr. Hyde*, Robert Louis Stevenson's melodrama. We still have a copy of the programme. It wasn't a romantic evening but it was the beginning. I fell. It was the best decision I ever made. Hormones again. Can God work through hormones? Why not? He invented them.

It was at this time that the telegram arrived announcing my father's death in action. *'The Admiralty deeply regrets...'* So did we, much more deeply. Barbara's presence and our growing love was a great help and she helped me work through the immediate grief but his death wasn't easy to cope with. It threw me off balance. The only exam I ever failed came shortly after this – for a University scholarship.

There seemed little reality about his death, happening so far away and with no tangible evidence. The truth was rammed home the day a small parcel arrived by post. In it was a pair of broken sweat-stained spectacles and a few other personal things. That was it but even then his death didn't seem real. For some years afterwards I had a recurring dream that he'd been found alive on a desert island and was coming back. The only emotion I don't remember feeling was anger. Not with the Japanese or the Admiralty, nor with the war.

A few miles from the church there was a large prisoner of war camp for German soldiers. As the war entered its final phases the authorities relaxed the restrictions and began to allow small groups of prisoners to attend local churches. I remember them grouped in the front pews. They wore drab uniforms with a circular patch of a different coloured cloth sewn into the back of their tunics for identification. They seemed to be human like we were and friendly, after the initial awkwardness. Although I didn't identify it at the time reconciliation was growing, even before the shooting stopped.

Later it went further. In 1949 two German students spent several weeks as part of our college campus. Like most of us they had served in the armed forces. I was part of the group that welcomed them. They went back to Germany and invited two of our students to return the visit. I was one of them, the other was John Sneath, who was to be the best man at our wedding. Our hosts included a man who'd served as an infantryman in the Wehrmacht and another who'd been a fighter pilot in the Luftwaffe and who had lost a leg after being shot down by the Royal Air Force. They had the same hopes for the future that we had, the same dreams of building bridges. We saw the merciless devastation that had been Hamburg. Almost four years after the war had ended the city was still in ruins. It was hard to rationalise the whole experience but like young men of any generation we put it out of conscious mind and accepted the friendship of the present.

Three years later during my second year in India I was invited to a Mission conference in Lucknow. I was asked to share a bedroom with another delegate. He proved to be a Japanese doctor. Somehow I felt no awkwardness with him. It helped me face and bury the hurts of war. He too had volunteered to work with leprosy sufferers. He too was a Christian.

As the Second World War entered its final phase I was deferred from conscription in order to sit university entrance exams. I was called up immediately after the war ended. Once I knew it was inevitable I volunteered for the Navy's medical corps. It seemed to me a better option to train to save life rather than to take it. Perhaps my father's death had something to do with the decision although I remember no conscious connection.

Basic training was at a requisitioned Butlin's holiday camp at Skegness. The camp's motto, carved in stone on the facade of the main building caused ribald comments each day as we doubled past it – *'Your Service Is Our Delight'*. The delight continued in another training centre on the coast of North Wales in February through a wicked winter. In spite of being trainee paramedics we learnt the skills of rifle maintenance and use – I became a skilled shot. We learned to throw hand grenades – a skill I couldn't understand as being very useful in the Navy. I thought the era of sailing ships and close boarding had finished with Nelson, although he seemed to be alive still in the minds of those who taught us. I also assumed that any enemy ship was unlikely to be closer than several miles and thus out of reach of even the most enthusiastic grenade thrower. We were also taught unarmed combat, a skill I only ever used once and effectively in India, but that's another story.

Our work included standing guard over the camp lavatories for four hours through the night. We had to account for their safety by assuring the officer of the watch that they were "All present and correct, Sir" whenever he tramped around. Which wasn't often. I suppose the presence and safety of lavatories would be important in time of war. Fear does strange things to the human body. More usefully, when he wasn't around I learnt to doze standing up without falling into the snow at my feet. When I was awake I wrote love letters to Barbara on the rough side of toilet paper with a blunt pencil in the faint light of a dim lamp.

We then went for nursing training as what was quaintly called Sick Berth Attendants. We were really male nurses. This took place in what had been a mental hospital and from which some of us thought the officers had graduated. With excellent grades I followed this up by taking specialist training which qualified me to work in operating theatres. After a time of practical experience at the Haslar Naval Hospital at Portsmouth I was stationed at a smaller but busy and happier hospital at Portland in Dorset.

Two of us were responsible for the work of the operating theatre together with a Queen Alexandra nursing sister and two Red Cross nurses. We had a varied menu of daily surgery. Routine appendectomies, gastric ulcers, hernias, varicose veins mainly on long-term sailors who'd stood around for too many years, orthopaedic work on injured backs and legs, and occasional burn victims from crashes on aircraft carriers. We were expected to do anything from preparing patients and instruments to scrubbing up each day and acting as assistants to the surgeons.

In my spare time I carried on reading. A friend and I received a regular monthly newsletter from Penguin Books from which we jointly ordered half a dozen paperbacks. We shared the reading and talked about them. It was better than the local pub where most of our mates ended up legless and broke.

Although the medical work was interesting, at the time I saw it as an unwelcome interruption in what I hoped to do – reading zoology and botany at university. Looking back I realise how valuable it was for my later life with The Leprosy Mission. I gained enough medical experience to understand the jargon and often to question what my medical colleagues thought and did.

But naval life and my engagement to Barbara changed my priorities. From sciences my interests moved into the arts and I settled for training as a school teacher at St. John's College, York. The thought of three years for a degree and a further year teacher training wasn't attractive. Few people married until they'd finished at university and found a job. We felt we'd waited long enough. It proved to be the right decision. If I'd taken the degree course I wouldn't have been qualified to offer myself for service with the Mission and the future would have been very different.

My main subjects were English Literature and the teaching of art, with theology (called Religious Knowledge then) as a subsidiary. St. John's was an Anglican foundation and had a great influence on me. It was a single sex college. Most of us were ex-servicemen. Older and more mature than most students, we were perhaps a little more determined to succeed.

This was in the late 1940s. The philosophy of art training could be summed up as 'Don't teach 'em anything, it might harm their creativity'. This applied not only to children in school but to the college students themselves. We had to make our own way. It was free but frustrating. No one taught us to draw and paint but we were still expected to produce a folio of finished work for assessment. A Distinction came my way in Finals. In my last year I edited the college magazine, maybe an early introduction to writing which was to mean so much many years later.

There were two other things for which I am still grateful. Both came from the College Principal, Canon Philip Lamb. First was his infectious enthusiasm for looking at the whole biblical story as a vast cosmic drama. God wasn't a puppet master pulling strings and moving people around on a stage but a powerful force for good, living and working through his people. As cynical students we were sometimes rebellious and critical but he fired my imagination, something very precious which has stayed with me through life.

The second gift he gave me was introducing me to what was then modern poetry, particularly T.S.Eliot. He helped me struggle with *The Wasteland* and other poems and set my mind ablaze with imagery. At times it was all random bits of jigsaw which only came together as a coherent whole years later.

Barbara and I were very much in love. We spent as much time together as we could during the college vacations. We cycled around Nottinghamshire and on one trip stopped at Southwell. We visited the Minster, a glory of Norman architecture with its statement of here-to-stay power and the more sophisticated beauty of its Early English chapter house.

In a side aisle we saw an exhibition by BELRA, the British Empire Leprosy Relief Association, now LEPRA. We knew nothing of leprosy and less of BELRA but we were gripped by a mock-up of an African village and the story of the suffering that leprosy could cause.

Back at college and preparing for Finals I was thinking and praying about our future. So was Barbara in Nottingham. We were young, we were Christian, we wanted to do something useful with our lives. I expected to go straight into teaching but the memory of the leprosy exhibition wouldn't leave me alone. I had an interest in modern art and a superficial knowledge of the influence African tribal art had had on artists like Picasso. Africa attracted me. Was God saying something? I didn't know, and our church wasn't the sort where people had visions or heard words direct from the Lord.

A few days later Barbara wrote to me about the exhibition suggesting we should think of working overseas. That was it. We wrote to BELRA but they told us courteously that they had no immediate use for our skills. They suggested that as we were Christian we should try The Mission to Lepers as it then was. We'd never heard of it. "Oh, I don't know. I'm not sure that's a good idea. They're a funny lot," said our minister when we spoke to him. It was an opinion based solely but justifiably on the Mission's local and rather eccentric representative, a man of strong, very narrow and voluble opinions.

If they were funny enough maybe they'd take us on. We wrote, offering our services for two years. The reply was encouraging but we were asked to consider a longer commitment. "You won't be much use for the first year or more. There's so much to learn." After interviews we were accepted. They *were* a funny lot. That proved it.

In later discussions Africa was ruled out, the Mission sent few people there. There was talk of Hong Kong, which attracted us but eventually we learned it was to be India. We'd not thought seriously about India at all although my grandfather had been a soldier there in Victorian days. When I was small he played marbles with me on the living room floor and told stories of shooting python and other tales. He never mentioned leprosy.

Noonday heat
Oils
1955

CHAPTER THREE

Innocents in India

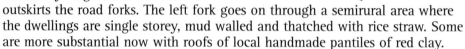

From Purulia town the rutted
road to the Leprosy Home passes
brick and plaster houses one or
two storeys high. At the town
outskirts the road forks. The left fork goes on through a semirural area where
the dwellings are single storey, mud walled and thatched with rice straw. Some
are more substantial now with roofs of local handmade pantiles of red clay.

Next it passes a fair-sized pond, the reflections of the houses and trees
disturbed each day by women washing clothes. Standing calf deep in the water,
saris hitched up to their knees, they beat the clothes on flat stones until the dirt
surrenders. Ducks, domesticated but slightly disgruntled, cruise sedately over the
water searching for frogs and small fish. The frogs and small fish search for
quiet places where there are no ducks or washerwomen. Later, when the sun has
warmed the water, people come to bathe. The ducks are chased out by laughing,
splashing children and disappear into the narrow lanes between the houses with
final disparaging twitches of the tail.

Again the road turns left and a few hundred yards later a shady avenue goes
off right. The trees are large, *pipal, banyan* and *nim*. Many bear the scars of
illicit chopping of branches for fuel but they arch over the road protectively. Past
the home for healthy children the road continues for half a mile through paddy
fields to the leprosy centre. The horizon is broken by a range of distant hills,
jungle-covered, shimmering blue in the heat haze.

The centre lies in an extensive compound of 150 acres. It had been built in a
grove of *sal* trees surrounded by more terraced paddy fields. Scattered among the
trees were more than 70 buildings. Among them were 40 three-roomed cottages
each fronted by a veranda and each room housing four patients. That was the
recognised number. Often there were more, depending on how many extra
patients in great need could be squeezed in.

One patient in each house was appointed *prachin – prachina* in the women's
houses – elders who were responsible for the welfare and behaviour of the other
eleven. The elders together formed a *panchayat* – a village style council – to
which were brought quarrels and disputes and which was always consulted
about major changes. As most changes were thought to be major it met every
Friday. Most were unsophisticated village people but they had wisdom, a natural
sense of justice and a great feeling of community.

As the Church Missionary Society folk moved out we took over. During the
war money hadn't been easy to find and there had been little scope for initiative.
Everything had been geared to survival. Many of the buildings were unkempt.
Little maintenance or improvement had been possible. Peeling plaster, rotting
window frames, black tidemarks where monsoon rain had run down the walls,
both outside and in. Between the houses, wherever there was space, patients

grew vegetables in straggling and untidy allotments. The whole place looked and felt tired.

Our remit was to build the place up to become a centre of excellence. It was a formidable challenge. Formal language learning over – although you never cease to absorb and learn another language and culture – we began to get to grips with the work. The school was working well and within two years I was asked to take over as Superintendent of the whole centre. I balked. I was a school teacher. I'd been in India less than two years. I'd had no training in management, but then neither had anyone else. There were two things in my favour. First there was no one else, a strong argument, and second I carried no baggage from the past. We were new. In the end and very reluctantly I agreed to do the job for six months until some one else could be found.

It became the best job in the world and I did it for 13 years. There was unfailing support from the Mission's leaders in the International Office in London. I was given a surprisingly free hand. I was so glad it took two weeks to get a reply to my letters and that telegrams were expensive and unreliable. This meant that I was able to use my initiative and make my own decisions before questions were asked or permission was granted or refused.

Where to begin in improving the patients' living conditions? After thought and consultation we decided that the key was food. Except for the children, the severely disabled and the acutely sick in the hospital wards, all the patients cooked their own food. They were given a weekly allowance of rice and a small sum of money, graded according to the work they did, to buy everything else from the centre's shop.

Occasionally two or three patients would cooperate and cook together but most did their own, making small clay fireplaces on the house verandas. Most had an inadequate diet although it was as good as they would have had in the villages they came from. The cooking produced Dickensian buildings with smoke-blackened walls and ceilings, and a never ending stream of seriously burnt fingers. A common effect of leprosy is the loss of sensation in the hands and feet. Damaged nerves don't transmit pain. Patients often thought it easier to pick up a burning coal fallen from the fire with fingers that didn't feel pain than to do it another way.

The answer was a central kitchen but when it was suggested to the elders there was opposition. This was change on a massive and emotional scale. Besides the other issues there was the question of community and caste. Most of our patients were Hindu, but there was a substantial minority of Christians and a small group of Muslims. Different groups didn't eat together. Even after leprosy had disrupted their place in society, patients still clung to their origins and customs. We had to persuade not compel.

I had taken over charge of the school from Mary Macdonald so she agreed to get the kitchen up and running. We installed simple stoves in a cleaned-up old building, found a couple of cooks and called for volunteers. About 35 patients agreed to give it a month's trial. They got three meals a day. A simple breakfast of *marbhat* – a rice gruel – and substantial meals at midday and early evening. It was usually rice and vegetable curry with egg, meat or fish once a week. This was better than a village diet, where meat would only be eaten at occasional celebrations – wedding feasts, the birth of a child, a funeral.

At the month's end few dropped out, more came in. It took a long time, we were feeling our way, but eventually so many people were eating from the 'hotel' that we were able to set a date for individual cooking to stop. We then faced the prospect of cleaning up the houses. We had a bricklayer and plasterer on the staff. We trained several others in the basics and let them loose on the older buildings, chipping off smoke-blackened, bedbug-ridden plaster and replacing it with new. Two staff carpenters worked with them. Many door and window frames were riddled with termites and crumbled when poked. I once suggested that most of our buildings would fall down if the white ants all died on the same day. It was their tunnels that held the walls together. I was only half joking.

Better living conditions and regular paint and colour washing did wonders for morale. The new kitchen meant that patients no longer needed to grow their own vegetables. We developed official gardens on a larger scale to supply the kitchen and to help the patients work more productively. We could also tidy up the areas around their cottages. Paths were put in, and the main 'roads' to the hospital block, church and other major buildings – then little more than rutted tracks – were consolidated and resurfaced.

Sanitation was primitive. Simple bore-hole latrines were located strategically but many patients preferred the village custom of an early morning walk to the fields. It was more sociable but hardly hygienic. We built water-flushed septic tank lavatories for everyone.

This required more water. We were dependent on surface wells, some of which dried up in the hot weather. Bill Bailey, the Mission's Field Secretary, fancied himself as a water diviner. He walked up and down with a forked stick cut from a tree, watched by wondering patients. I was sceptical. I felt that wherever we dug in Purulia if we dug deep enough we'd find water, but he was the boss.

We chose two sites. One was in the middle of the compound where we could also build a water tower, the other some distance away in the rice fields. This was lower down and nearer a natural drainage area. Work began at the start of the hot weather in April. At this time ground water levels are at their lowest and least likely to interfere with the digging. We needed holes about 16 feet in diameter to give a substantial well after the brickwork was in place. How deep depended on finding water. It was usually at around 50 feet and the excavation was all done by hand. We had no machines; just a block and tackle to lift heavy baskets of soil and rock to the surface.

The well in the compound progressed quickly. The other was difficult. Very soon a stratum of rock appeared and further digging was hampered by its hardness. There were no easy methods. The rock was split by chisel and sledge hammer. Below the rock layer we found an abundant stream of water much too near the surface. In spite of this water we needed to go much deeper to ensure a reliable supply all the year round. By degrees, bailing out and smashing rock we sank the well further. By the end of May we were making good progress again.

The monsoon usually began about the middle of June so we had two weeks to raise the brickwork in each well to clear the expected water level. As the well floors were cleared, and masons and bricks were lowered on pulleys, ominous clouds gathered. In a couple of days the rains had broken – two weeks early. The water level in each well began to rise as torrential storms hit the area. We had no chance with the well in the rice fields. It had to be left. We concentrated on the excavation in the compound. Three six-hour shifts worked each day. The patients responded. They understood the need for water and weren't prepared to waste the great efforts they'd already made. It was most impressive at night. There were 30 or more men on the surface, sweating bodies glistening in the light of kerosene lamps as they lowered baskets of bricks and mortar down the dark hole at their feet to a dozen men below. The noise could be heard for miles.

Well digging in progress, Purulia, 1954

The wall rose, the water followed. Each day brought its rain storm and the water level pursued the bricklayers in a dramatic race. When the depth of the water measured ten feet the brickwork measured thirteen. Two more days and the danger was past. The well wall was bricked up to ground level. We'd won. The spirit of the patients was amazing. These were 'outcasts', folk who'd been marked out and rejected by their communities because of their illness. They'd responded to a challenge with determination and humour. They'd not only beaten the weather, in a real sense they'd beaten leprosy too. By their own efforts they'd found new courage and self-worth. This was a transformation we saw many times and from which the awe never disappeared. It was the recreation of human dignity.

News from the other well in the paddy fields wasn't so good. Overnight a tremendous storm broke and the well was flooded almost to the surface. Reluctantly we put up a framework of bamboo and corrugated iron to protect it as much as we could and left it. One day it might be possible to complete it but not now.

Slowly, over a period of several years the centre began to look like and function as a well-organised medical centre. The International Office in London recruited more medical and nursing staff to work with us. We agreed a planned programme of modernisation with them. The renovation of old buildings gave way to the building of new ones. At first we used an Indian civil engineer and a team of skilled masons from north India. The contractor, Mr. Agrawal was a large but gently spoken man, a Hindu with a real sense of service. His buildings were well and honestly made but as time passed I began to feel that I'd learnt enough to do my own work. I drew my own blueprints for new wards, taking the technical details from the plans produced for earlier buildings. I estimated costs and began to build. The wards didn't fall down, no one got hurt and we saved a third of the money.

The most ambitious project I did in this way was to design and build the planned water tower beside the new well. It was to hold about 10,000 gallons of water and was of brick and reinforced concrete. That amount of water is colossally heavy and we built the tower strong. Once completed we installed a petrol driven pump, connected the pipes and began to fill the tank 25 feet above ground level. There was a great deal of spontaneous

Purulia Rice Fields
Oils
1960

prayer. There were no leaks, no cracks, no accidents. The tower and a second one in another part of the hospital are still in use 40 years later.

The rains affected life in other ways. They flooded animals out of their burrows and made them seek drier accommodation elsewhere. Like our bathroom. We always shook out our shoes in the morning before putting them on our feet. There could be bugs, even frogs, taking temporary refuge inside. One morning I forgot to shake out my shirt which had hung all night on a clothes hook. As I put it on there was a sudden excruciating flash of pain down my back. I let out a howl that could have been heard for miles and dropped the shirt. Barbara rushed in. In the shirt folds on the floor was a scorpion. Barbara, protecting her own, crushed it with a sandalled foot.

I'd been stung three times in the moment it had taken me to get the shirt off my back. The pain was intense. The medics offered sympathy and assured me I'd be all right in several hours time. Small comfort. I took out the Land Rover and drove out down the road and continued driving for an hour or so until the pain became bearable. It was something to do. I survived.

Snakes were another matter. We had a wickerwork stool in the bathroom. Drying herself after a bath one day Barbara put her foot on the stool and moved it. There was a strange feel to it, a sort of resistance as it slid over the polished cement floor. She lifted it up. Coiled inside was two feet of *krait*, black in colour and banded in white. One of India's most poisonous snakes. Fortunately it was sleepy. It had got in through the drain that let out the bath water. With great aplomb Barbara wrapped herself in a towel, walked into the bedroom and called for help.

On another occasion we were driving home in the dusk after an evening meal with friends. As we approached our garden gate I stopped the Land Rover. Barbara got out and went to release the catch on the top bar. I switched on the headlights to help her see. Just below her hand was another *krait*.

I kept a long and heavy stick near the front door of the bungalow. It was my snake stick and I carved a notch on it for each snake I killed. I'd seen too many cowboy films. But my conscience began to make me uncomfortable. I was sure some of the snakes I killed were not poisonous and were of no danger. One day I saw a newspaper advert. '*Bombay Natural History Society. Chart for Identifying Poisonous and Non-poisonous Snakes. Two Rupees.*' I sent for it.

It arrived a few days later. A folded double page of words and pictures. The first instruction read: '*Count the number of scales between the snake's eye and nostril.*' There followed details to help identify the various species we might expect to see. Cobras, *kraits*, rat snakes, whatever. The second paragraph began: '*Turn the snake over to see its underside.*' "Great," I thought. "When I do that, will the snake know that it's all for its good and cooperate?" It was an interesting chart but not much use in my small attempt at conservation.

CHAPTER FOUR

Christmas in Purulia

Most of this development was without electricity. There was a small and erratic electricity supply company in Purulia town but it was functioning at its limit with old generators and we were too far out of town anyway. It would have been too expensive to pay for several miles of posts and overhead wires to the hospital. But it was hard running a hospital without it. There was no power for X-ray machines, only hurricane lanterns in the wards and pressure lamps in the operating theatre and elsewhere.

Then came a State Government project bringing power from a new dam built 40 miles away. We watched with growing anticipation as the line of pylons gradually snaked across the fields. It passed less than a mile from the hospital and after battling through a morass of red tape we were able to make a connection. It made a great difference. Proper lighting everywhere. Power for X-ray, air conditioning in the major operating theatre and much more.

We always staged a nativity play at Christmas. It was a joint effort by staff and patients, adults and children. When our first Christmas with electricity came, we decided the play would be the biggest and the best we'd ever put on. It would be out in the open air and in the evening so that we could make full use of the new lighting. We built an earth stage on a wide stretch of flat ground and erected a makeshift proscenium arch over it, all bamboo and jute sacking. We made footlights out of old kerosene tins and lined them across the stage.

In the planning group someone said, "As it's outside let's have a real fire for the shepherds to sit around." It was a great idea which began to expand under its own impetus. "What about real sheep?" That was easy. We could borrow a dozen from the nearby village. And although we didn't recognise it that's where the trouble began.

In rehearsal the sheep began to stray looking for food. We chopped up straw for them and spread it around on the ground. They ate it quickly and strayed some more. Then came another idea. "Let's tie string around the necks of the sheep and each shepherd can hold two or three of them. The strings won't be seen in the dark." It seemed to work.

My idea was the one that did it. Near the stage was the central kitchen. It had a flat roof. I suggested that we put up a ladder against the far side of the kitchen. The angels, all children in white robes and silver wings, could climb up quietly in the dark and line up on the roof edge. At the appropriate moment we could switch on the floodlights, kept in reserve for the occasion. The angels would suddenly appear as though flying through the dark night sky, the stars behind them. It was high drama.

Came the evening of the play. The air was taut with excitement. Almost all the patients gathered, Hindu, Muslim, Christian. The staff were there in force and so were many folk from the neighbouring villages. There was just one thing we hadn't taken into account in our planning. That was the sheep's reaction when the lights suddenly flashed on and the angels appeared from nowhere. The stage was flooded in light and so was the heavenly host. "Baaa," went the sheep. "Fear not," shouted the angels from on high. "Baaaa," went the sheep. "We bring you good tidings of great joy," shouted the angels. In Bengali of course. "Baaaaa," went the sheep and one, even more terrified than the rest, backed into the fire.

Its tail began to burn. It bleated once more, jumped about a foot in the air, wrenched its string from the shepherd's restraining hand and leapt into the dark. All the other sheep followed. Within seconds there were a dozen panic-stricken sheep dashing through an audience of a thousand people sitting cross-legged in the dark. It was pandemonium. Some made valiant attempts to catch the sheep, grasping wildly as living legs of mutton dashed by. It was in vain. It took us almost 24 hours to track down the last sheep. I don't remember how we finished the play. My mind has blanked it out. It wasn't the best nativity play we ever produced but it's the one we all remember.

Christmas in Purulia was always a wonderful experience. Somehow barriers came down and most people joined in. Our main Carol Service was on Christmas Eve. The hospital church was spacious, built by an earlier generation of workers in pseudo-Gothic style. Arched windows, buttresses and even a small bell tower. It made no compromise with Indian architectural forms or customs, except that the congregation sat on mats on the floor. I guess that was more to avoid the expense of pews rather than respect for local culture. Even after the advent of electricity we continued the tradition of a candle-lit service, with scores of candles on wooden brackets around the church. The flickering flames painted the walls gently in soft light, reflecting from the faces of the congregation, pushing mysterious shadows high into the roof. We could almost see the angels lurking in the rafters. It was usually a lovely service, with a mixture of indigenous

Christmas carol singing in Purulia

Bengali carols and translations from English, all led by the children. In early days the singing was unaccompanied but later we had tablas, Indian drums and cymbals. Earlier generations of missionaries had rejected these instruments as Hindu. We came to think of them simply as Indian and accepted them. They made a great difference to the singing.

The carol service didn't always go as planned. Occasionally Naomi disrupted it. She was a sad patient in her thirties. Her leprosy was healed but she was already disabled and had been rejected by her family. To add to her sufferings she was mentally unstable. She caused problems at the Home, but there was nowhere else she could go. At times she erupted into violence and had to be restrained. In Indian village tradition that meant manacles on her hands and chains on her ankles. It was a solution which had been used in desperation even in the Leprosy Home but in our day we firmly ruled it out. However, there were still times when she had to be confined to a locked room. The nearest mental hospital was 70 miles away and was always full. It served a population of millions and had even greater demands on its services than a leprosy centre.

It was the changing seasons that seemed to trigger Naomi's mental illness. It was signalled more than once by her sudden appearance at the carol service. The candles brought something out in her and she would walk around the walls speaking unintelligibly and systematically blowing out the flames. The children thought it was great fun. The tragedy of it escaped them.

Eventually we managed to negotiate a place for her in the mental hospital hoping she might get some effective treatment. The problem was getting her through the three-hour car journey, 70 miles on a bad road. She was sedated. She slept all the way on a mattress in the back of the Land Rover and the journey was peaceful. The mental hospital kept her for three months then sent her back to us without any warning, saying there was nothing they could do for her. Months later after going through a quiet patch Naomi became hard to handle once more. One day several of us were watching a football match between two teams of patients. Naomi stood in front of us staring wildly. She accused us of poisoning her. She was referring to the sedation she'd been given to get her through the journey. "You poisoned me," she said, "and I died and went to heaven. I saw Matthew, Mark, Luke and John." She paused, pointed a finger at us and emphasised, "but I didn't see any of you there." I guess she was right. Innocent sufferers like Naomi will find a place in the Kingdom before many of us.

Christmas Day was quiet. There was a short service in the morning, a quick round of the hospital wards by the doctors, another by Barbara and me to wish everyone a *Baradiner namaskar* – Christmas Greetings – and then we all relaxed at home.

Another annual highlight was the *prem bhoj*, the love feast. It was really a Christmas dinner to which everyone of whatever faith was invited and to which all came in friendship. A couple of days after Christmas the hospital football field was cleared and cooking pits dug at the side under the shade of a clump of trees. Early in the morning a gang of men began work preparing rice, meat and vegetable curries for more than 600 patients. The staff and child patients served

Preparing the Christmas love feast at Purulia

and although there was no compulsion and no pressure almost all the patients came. It looked a bit like the feeding of the 5,000 although in our scenario the miracle was that the food was always ready on time.

The patients sat on the grass and ate from banana leaf plates. Cleaning up afterwards was no problem. As the meal progressed hordes of large black crows began to assemble and quarrel with hungry, half wild *pi* dogs. Larger kites swooped down, scooping titbits from under the dogs' noses. Between them they left nothing but the leaves which were quickly hauled away.

There were occasional challenges. We gave the contract to supply the meat, always goat, to a pair of Muslim butchers. They drove in several live animals and turned them into meat on the spot. Life was basic. There were no hygienic supermarkets. Meat came in skins not in plastic wrappers. One Christmas the two butchers quarrelled. We never found out why but suddenly there was a fight. One man had insulted the other and probably all his family for the previous six generations and was confronting him with great drama. The other was brandishing a large sharp butcher's knife in his hand, hysterical with anger and ready to use it. It was serious.

Without thinking - if I'd thought I wouldn't have done it - I stepped in between the two and slapped the man who'd done the insulting. He staggered and fell down, more from surprise than from the force of the blow. I turned quickly to the other man, grabbed the wrist of the hand that held the knife and pulled him across my body so that he faced away from me. My other arm locked round his neck, hard.

There was a sudden stunned silence. Everyone froze. It looked like that game of statues we used to play as children – when the whistle blew we all had to stand still in whatever attitude we'd adopted. I yelled for someone to grab the knife. No one moved. I tightened my grip, I didn't really know what else to do. Then one of the staff moved, prised the knife out of the man's hand and the tension was over. We sent the two men off in different directions to cool off. I hoped my trembling didn't show. I began to see the point of vegetarianism, although I suppose you can quarrel violently over potatoes if the mood takes you. It was the only time my naval unarmed combat training ever came in handy. I've never been terribly keen on the Church Militant.

The Christmas Sports Day really wound up the festivities. Children and adults took part with events for all sorts and conditions of men and women. It included a slow cycle ride in which the last person over the finishing line won, and which tended to last a long time. There was also an Elephant Stampede. That wasn't its official title but it describes what happened. Many patients suffered from plantar ulcers, a common complication in leprosy which severely damages their feet. The most effective treatment then was a below-knee plaster of Paris cast with a wooden rocker sole to aid walking. It was all very heavy. It immobilised the foot, spread the body's weight evenly and provided the conditions in which the foot could rest and ulcers heal. Until Sports Day that was.

Determined not to be left out of the fun and prizes, patients with plaster casts had their own 50 yard flat race. We expected it to be a rather sedate affair in which the winner limped home a little faster than the slow cycle ride. Nothing of the sort. They galloped, thumping down the hard track with their bandaged legs. Elephants would have been quieter and a little bit faster but there was no denying the determination and the spirit. The doctors tended to look away.

Indian Village
Watercolour
1960

CHAPTER FIVE

Sadhu

Sashibhusan Patnaik – the Sadhu. c.1960

Shashibhusan – Shashi - came to Purulia in our early years. Tall, thin almost to emaciation, he had a well-worn face and close-cropped hair. He wore the saffron robes of the *sadhu*, a Hindu holy man. Born into a middle-class family in Orissa, he'd been educated up to university standard although failing his final exams in chemistry. Then came signs of leprosy.

His family supported him but for two or three years he stayed at home, rarely venturing outside the family courtyard. No one should know their shame. He tried whatever treatments he could find but nothing worked. The disease progressed. Shashi was a devout Hindu believing in reincarnation. Some held that leprosy was a curse from God. His own tradition taught that his illness was a consequence of actions in a past life, unknown and unknowable but real. Everything that happened to him in his present life was *karma*, the working out of the past.

He was disturbed and desperate. Perhaps a pilgrimage would please the gods. He put on the saffron, the deep orange robes of a spiritual pilgrim. Over the next couple of years he wandered through India. He walked the roads, visiting the major holy sites of Hinduism. He prayed for blessing, for some sign to encourage him. Eventually it came but not in a way he could ever have imagined. His leprosy deteriorated and was becoming more obvious. His hands were weakening and beginning to claw, the balance of muscles changing through damage to the nerves that control them. In desperation he came to Purulia to see if he could find help at the leprosy centre. He was fortunate. He came on a day when there was room. He was admitted.

His treatment was stabilised and his general health improved. We had to find him work, something to occupy his mind, to take his thoughts off himself and his illness. Better educated than most patients we asked him to supervise the workers in one of the large vegetable gardens. He reorganised it. Then he took over the hospital flower garden. He was thoughtful and cooperative and enthusiastic in everything he did. He still wore saffron and he maintained one quiet day a week for meditation when he wouldn't speak to anyone, whatever the provocation. In an emergency he'd write a note but even that was exceptional. We accepted this, respecting him for himself.

Among the other patients with whom he shared a ward were two young Christian men, Cornelius and Rajen. These were the two young school teachers mentioned earlier and who were still patients at this time. Shashi began to talk to them about their faith. They suggested he go with them to church. It interested him and he began asking questions. They could usually give answers but Shashi wasn't easy to satisfy and occasionally they came to me for advice about what to say.

I kept a prayerful distance. I felt it was far better for them to continue to talk to Shashi rather than take the initiative myself. I've always believed that whenever possible evangelism is best performed low key and by people firmly rooted in the local soil. Foreigners, however well meaning, often have an imperfect grasp of local culture and the nuances of language. And in any case I couldn't speak as someone who'd gone through the trauma of leprosy. They could.

He had many questions. The concept of a God who offers wholeness and health and who doesn't visit illness on individuals wasn't easy to take in. Nor was the assurance of forgiveness. He took time digesting all this and more. Eventually Shashi came to a crisis point. He asked for baptism. Shanti Babu, the ordained Indian pastor who worked with us began to take him through the standard instruction. Shashi grew impatient. One morning he confronted me. "I believe," he said. "When may I be *Christ* - ened?" He put all the emphasis of the

English word (he spoke English fluently) on *Christ.* He wanted to be like Christ.

He was baptised publicly in the open-air baptistery in the church garden. It was called the *Church of the Good Samaritan.* He continued to wear his saffron robes. It was unusual for a Christian but it didn't disturb me. They were still a

Purulia Leprosy Hospital Church –
the Church of the Good Samaritan, 1955

sign of a man pursuing holiness and they were part of his personality. Why should he be asked to conform to other people's standards? He also carried on with his quiet days, but he also began an active witness, both one to one with other patients and through his preaching in the church. He had a new assurance. The stammer which was very noticeable when he was at all tense almost disappeared when he preached.

He grew in stature. For some time I'd been developing a small pottery within the centre. A few patients were *kumar*, potters by caste and trade, and I encouraged their skills in making red earthenware cooking pots, water jars and pantiles for sale. One man had modelling skills and I suggested he model a few animals – horses, cattle, elephants. We fired them in a simple kiln alongside the pots, painted them briskly and began to sell them to visitors. The pottery grew bigger. We recruited more potters. I made contact with a Cottage Industries Emporium in Calcutta, 200 miles away and they agreed to buy from us.

As the pottery grew it needed some organisational skills. Shashi took it over. We began to talk about further developments. Could we build better kilns and start to make glazed pottery? It sounded ambitious. I had a book – I always seem to have a book – which gave some basic theory and information about the chemical formulae for glazes. Remembering his chemistry he was intrigued. It sounded possible. It was worth a try.

So began months of experiment. He tried different formulae, redesigned and modified our simple kilns. They didn't work. Occasionally there was a glimmer of hope but not enough. He got depressed. Then one morning he burst into my office. "I have it," he said, a modern Archimedes shouting *Eureka*. "This will work." A new idea had come to him, he said, in a God-given dream.

A couple of days later he held in his hand a shining pot, still warm from the kiln. It wasn't perfect,

Purulia Pottery, 1960

but it was glazed. Within weeks he and his potters were producing beautiful glazed pots in cobalt blues, copper greens and other colours, each one an individual creation. He called his combination of chemicals *The Saviour's Constitution,* and for several years we continued to supply pottery to outlets in Calcutta and other places.

Later, home on leave in England after we'd developed the pottery further, I bought *The Potter's Handbook* by Bernard Leach, a famous artist potter. Reading it I learnt that we had rediscovered *raku*, an ancient Japanese method of pottery glazing. If we'd had the book earlier we could have saved time but we wouldn't have had the thrill it gave us to know what we'd done.

Eventually with the dramatic changes in the treatment of leprosy most patients were able to take treatment at home in their own communities and the pottery was closed. It had served its purpose. Before that happened Shashi had improved medically to the point where doctors and the laboratory declared him negative, symptom-free. We were too cautious in those days to say *cured*, we used the phrase *disease arrested*. But his hands were still clawed.

At this time Paul Brand* was making waves in the leprosy world in south India and beyond. His new vision and original techniques of tendon transplantation were bringing new hope to disabled leprosy sufferers. They could restore function to useless hands and make the damage less obvious, but the surgery needed good pre- and post-operative physiotherapy, something quite new in leprosy.

Kenneth Kin Thein was another patient, a young educated Burmese Christian who'd worked in All India Radio before leprosy hit him. We asked if he'd go to work with Paul Brand and his team in the Christian Medical College Hospital at Vellore. It was a thousand miles away but we needed someone to train in basic physiotherapy. He agreed. When he returned to Purulia after training he set up a small physio department. He began an uphill struggle to teach sceptical patients that their physical disabilities could be improved with exercises and wax bath therapy. It wasn't easy combating generations of belief in the inevitability of the damage leprosy did but he made progress.

With our doctors' agreement I wrote and invited Paul Brand to visit Purulia to demonstrate his techniques. He came and ours was the first hospital outside Vellore to open its own reconstructive surgical unit. Paul came with Ruth Thomas, the English physiotherapist who had trained Kenneth. We didn't know at the time that Kenneth and Ruth had fallen in love. Eventually they married and returned to Burma where they gave a lifetime of service to leprosy patients, but that's another story.

The next problem was finding volunteers to undergo this surgery. There were many patients who needed it but it was all too new. To them it was untried and in honesty we couldn't promise perfect results. Shashi led the way, the first to volunteer for surgery. Weeks later the results were good. His hand wasn't perfect cosmetically, but it was stronger, more mobile and a working hand again. This success broke the ground and we had no more difficulty finding patients for operation.

Shashi's skills were too valuable to lose. As he no longer needed treatment I offered him a position on the staff as my assistant. It was one of the first appointments of ex-patients on to the staff of a leprosy hospital and we worked together as friends, trying out new ideas on each other and continuing to develop the work and witness of the centre.

At the Mission's Centenary in 1974 Shashi was invited to London to speak about his experiences at a number of meetings throughout the UK. He enjoyed it although he was appalled at British wealth and waste. We took him for a short break to a friend's holiday cottage in the Lake District. The idea of someone

---

* His story is well known and is told in *Ten Fingers for God* by Dorothy Clarke.

having two fully equipped homes, one of which was empty for months at a time was more than he could take. But there were many more positive things, and moments of fun. Sitting in my car one day we were held up at a school crossing by a lollipop lady carrying her sign which said 'Stop – Children'. He asked what it was. I convinced him it was part of the British family planning campaign. He was impressed and thought the idea might be used in India.

He continued at Purulia for the rest of his working life, eventually giving up the saffron robe, marrying and adopting an orphan boy whom they named Napoleon. I never understood why he chose that name, but without all the baggage of British history I guess he saw Napoleon as a man who fought his way to the top against the odds. In his final years Shashi went blind but his faith never wavered. We can forgive him for calling his son Napoleon.

Sashi, during a visit to London in 1974, with Barbara and Jenny

Tibetan Buddhist shrine
Watercolour
1960

CHAPTER SIX

Simonpur

A grove of *sal* trees stands straight and tall in the heat on the north-western edge of the hospital compound. Just beyond them the paddy fields begin. The field edges are raised to hold the rainwater in the monsoon growing season and go down in steps of about two feet. This allows the lower fields to be watered by gravity from those above. They reach their lowest point about half a mile away. For most of the year the fields are barren, the earth fissured and cracked, the dusty gold stubble from last year's rice crop waiting to be ploughed in when the first rain softens the ground in early June.

It's a time of promise, if the rains begin. Out come wooden ploughs with a six-inch tip of locally-fashioned iron. It's an ancient design. I've seen similar ones in the Cairo Archaeological Museum, 3,000 years old although without the iron tip. Pairs of scrawny bullocks or heftier black water buffalo are yoked up and the earth is turned over. A scatter of white egrets follow the plough, high stepping through the clods, picking up lunch, occasionally flapping into the air in a flurry of feathers.

It's here that the other well was dug and abandoned when it flooded in the early rains. The following year we tried again. The hot weather gained hold, each day 110°F and more in the shade. The sun leached all the colour from the landscape. It pressed down on us and the slightest physical activity became an effort. Even sound seemed muted in the heat, deadened and dull. We trundled out an old three-horsepower petrol-driven pump on its iron chassis. Manhandling it over the rough ground and down the terraces, we installed it near the well and began to pump out the water.

We began work early in the morning to avoid the hottest part of the day and at first we seemed to be gaining on the water level. Then the pump broke down. Our mechanic dismantled part of it, located the problem and we began again. He hand cranked the engine several times. It coughed, burst into life but with the feeling in his hands damaged by leprosy he lost hold of the loose crank handle. It began to rotate at several hundred revs per minute on the flywheel. Not fancying several pounds of steel flying off and hitting one of us in the face, we dived for cover until the mechanic crawled up and stopped the engine.

The pump couldn't do the job on its own. It couldn't control the flow of water. Since the advent of electricity we'd put an electric submersible pump in the successful well in the centre. We decided to bring this over to add to the effort we were making. We drew overhead copper wires to bring current over the fields. Our poles were bamboo with wooden cross pieces holding the usual white porcelain insulators and included an earth wire running down the last pole. The combined efforts of the two pumps brought the water level right down. We managed several more feet of digging and began making a permanent job of it by bricking up the side walls.

Halfway through, one of the patients working in the well came up for a breather. Soaking wet and tired he leant one arm on the bamboo pole with the earth wire. There was a grunt. He flew through the air and landed unconscious on the ground, electrocuted. We rushed him back to the hospital where he spent a night in bed and by next morning was enjoying the hospital food. There were no more accidents and the well was soon ready for use. Fools rush in. I don't mean the patients, but I think I came into that category.

We shared the water with folk living nearby. Their village lay another half mile up the far slope of the fields, on the crest of the land. It looked like any other of the thousands of villages that punctuate the rural landscape of West Bengal. A cluster of single-storey mud-walled cottages, roofs thatched in grey-gold or covered in deep red ochre pantiles. They jostled for space with little room for expansion except at the edge of the village. Cottage walls were neatly hand-plastered with a mixture of the local clay and fresh cow dung. There was never any shortage of that and it dried to a hard, water-resistant protection for the mud walls. As the weather began to cool after each rainy season the women would repair any damaged walls and then decorate the outside of the houses.

Combining the plaster mixture with deep red clay or black powder paint they'd cover the walls with intricate, semi-abstract designs based on the rice plant and the lotus. Sometimes whole walls were covered. Others, less creative, simply dipped a hand into whitewash and printed a whole line of white palm prints round the doors and windows to ward off the evil eye. A few would express themselves more elaborately, painting a tiger or an elephant on the wall. In later years these were often supplemented with written graffiti saying *Vote CPI(M)* – the Communist Party of India (Marxist) – or some other political party. West Bengal is one of the few Indian States which has had a democratically elected Communist government in power for some years.

The houses and courtyards were close together and eccentric paths zigzagged between them, some just wide enough to take a bullock cart, others purely pedestrian. But it was a village with a difference. A thousand people lived there at the start of our association with them and eventually two thousand. All had unwelcome connections with leprosy. Some had active disease but didn't want the constraints of living in the hospital centre and chose to live near enough to attend as outpatients. Others had been asked to leave the centre because of anti-social behaviour, leprosy sufferers being human like the rest of us. Many were disease arrested but for personal reasons settled in the village rather than face the prospect of going back home. Some had never had the illness but were part of the family of a patient who had.

The village was called Simonpur, the village of Simon. It was named after Simon in the New Testament, a man who entertained Jesus in his home in Bethany and whom Jesus healed of leprosy. The local owner of the land had allowed a few patients to settle there decades earlier and the village had simply grown. Attractive though it looked, life was very hard and basic for most of the inhabitants. A few had a regular income, their families sending them rice or small sums of money to keep them away from home. Most were on or below the breadline.

The main source of income was begging. In the festival seasons, Hindu, Muslim or Christian, the village would be almost deserted. Just a few of the elderly together with older children were left to care for the cattle, goats and chickens. The rest would scatter over a wide area going into the major towns, bandaged and be-crutched. The more extreme their disabilities – real or pretended – the more likely they were to gain the sympathy of the alms-giving public. At slack times the village was crowded with men, women and bright-eyed children.

There were other marginal sources of income even less desirable than begging. A few brewed illicit liquor. Drugs were peddled – a bandaged leprosy patient was not likely to be taken into custody by the police and thoroughly searched – and prostitution was a sideline for one or two. Occasionally, although not very often, a few of the more enterprising would make a night-time raid on the leprosy centre's ponds to take a few fish with throw nets.

The village had usually been looked on by the hospital staff as a bit of a nuisance. It sometimes was, but there were many people in real need of help. Walking through the village the plight of the children hit hard. Most were malnourished and vulnerable to the common and dangerous childhood illnesses. And what of their future? With little chance of education they had no way out of the cycle of poverty and deprivation they'd been born into. We wondered if a more positive approach might secure more cooperation.

We began a twice-weekly visit to the village to dispense medicine for leprosy and common minor ailments, and held dressing clinics for those with ulcers. Eventually we put up a small permanent building in village style, mud walls and tiles. At the same time we gave powdered milk and vitamins to the children, arranged vaccination programmes and began to admit a few seriously ill folk to the hospital.

Marian, our senior nursing sister, took great interest in the people. Among other things she began an informal weekly worship service with a small group of Christians there. One day she came to see me, her face wreathed in smiles.

"They want a church," she said.

"Who do?"

"The people in Simonpur."

"Great," I said.

"When can we start to build it?" she asked. "Look."

She held out her hand. In it was a small collection of copper coins, worth about sixpence in old British currency, two and a half pence decimal. Not much, but it was the first time beggars had offered anything back.

"When can *we* build it?" I responded. "Why should *we* build it?"

She was speechless.

"Look," I said, "these folk make their living by begging. It's not a great way to live, not much self-esteem in it. Encourage them to build the church themselves. If they want it badly enough they'll do it. And when it's finished it'll be theirs."

She wasn't happy. We talked it through. As far as I was concerned it was being hard to be kind. The Christians too took some convincing but over the next few months they found a small vacant plot of land near the village centre and began to put up mud walls. It took a lot of labour but it didn't need money, just days of noisy argument. When the walls were high enough I gave them a couple of old window frames and a door and as it got to roof level we relented enough to give them the tiles. When it was completed it was their church. The one they'd argued, quarrelled and sweated over, and it was complete. They'd done it and they were proud of it.

The Church for Sixpence, Simonpur, 1982

Over the years little gifts were made. A wooden cross, a rickety table to put it on, a few cotton mats to sit on. It's still a simple basic building but it's used regularly and cared for. We call it *The Church for Sixpence*. The Church for Two and a Half New Pence somehow doesn't sound so good.

I took the same approach when the expanding population needed another well. I refused to do it for them and challenged them to help themselves. They had to decide where to dig it and how to organise the voluntary labour. But wells are more expensive than simple church buildings so we reached an agreement. Once it was dug and showing promise the hospital would supply them with bricks. In later years, after Barbara and I had left India, Rudi Stein and his wife It, Dutch workers with the Mission, took more interest in Simonpur's people and helped them to locate two tube wells in the village. The result of having covered, uncontaminated clean water was to reduce the amount of gastroenteric illness – diarrhoea, dysentery and other upsets – by nearly 50 per cent.

We also began to employ a few of the villagers. We trained three men as bricklayers to work on repairs to our buildings. We took several others with a little more education to train as nurse aides and paramedical workers and gave casual work to a number who harvested our rice crop each year.

Today the village is more prosperous. It has a thriving school and a couple of shops. Begging is very much a minority activity and a few television aerials can be seen sprouting from the bigger houses. Two or three of the younger, brighter folk – a young woman and two young men – have struggled their way through to university and proudly claim their BAs.

A little further away lay another village, Sonajhuri. Some nights around the time of village festivals we'd hear the drums from there. It signalled *Chou Nach*, a tradition of dance, centuries old. The dancers were professionals who travelled the countryside performing wherever they could find an audience.

We'd follow the bobbing hurricane lamps as people wove their way through the velvet darkness of an Indian night to the dance site, an open patch of ground on the edge of the village. Crowds pushed and jostled with great good nature around the sweetmeat stalls, rapidly set up for business. Sweet orange

jelabis, even sweeter *rasagula*, roast peanuts in conical bags twisted from old newspapers, all lit fitfully by smoking paraffin lamps. In a corner, behind makeshift screens the dancers would begin their make up. An elaborate confection of greasepaint and paper masks, peacock feather head-dresses, multicoloured sequinned satin and tinsel costumes.

Above, drumming for the Chou Nach; right, a dancer makes up for the Chou Nach, 1982

The drums began. Great bass drums reverberated. They were four feet across, goat skins stretched taut over wooden frames. Smaller drums spelled out a complex rhythm. They played on and on, building an atmosphere of great expectation. Suddenly, when least expected, a figure leaps out of the darkness into the glare of the hissing pressure lanterns. He is a mythical figure, posturing, threatening, demanding attention. The crowd quietens except for the wail of a baby. There's a crash of cymbals and a second dancer confronts the first. A long, drawn-out, high-stepping fight begins. They whirl around each other, wooden swords hissing through the air. Their shadows too appear to fight. They skim the ground, contorted, blurred, now sharp, merging with the darkness. Then one figure falls. He's dead. It's over. The audience sighs collectively. Evil has been defeated.

There's a pause. The figure lies still. The drums quicken and another dancer struts into the light. He's dressed as a bird, a vulture. No, not dressed as, he *is* a vulture. He moves with a curious grace, every gesture birdlike. His arms are ruffling wings, his neck stretching out, his steps slow and cautious. He approaches the figure on the ground, circles, waits. Yet another dancer enters, a hyena. They fight briefly then together they drag the body away. Their movements are full of observation, brimming with conviction. Their raw energy has a wild beauty about it. Slowly the story unfolds. A tale of mythical beings, saints and sinners, good and evil. It goes on for several hours almost till dawn when, as in all good stories, virtue finally triumphs. The drums are silent and the drummers, sleek with sweat, can rest. The crowd drifts away quietly, satisfied, young children asleep and slumped over fathers' shoulders, mothers walking behind.

Leprosy beggars
Watercolour
1960

CHAPTER SEVEN

Pressures Build

Voices were raised under the
banyan tree outside the treatment
centre. It was an old tree, spreading
shade across the road, offering
temporary shelter to patients sitting
on its roots. It was an early morning in November 1950. The sky was blue, still
pale and cool, the air fresh. The hot weather had given way to the rains. Now
they too had gone, together with their mixed blessings of water, high humidity
and the intense irritation of prickly heat no matter how frequently I bathed or
showered. We rejoiced simply in the absence of heat. The emerald green of the
paddy fields was turning slowly to gold and harvest was almost upon us.

   Noise seemed to carry further in the cool air, each sound clear and distinct.
The loud voices were not quarrels, just friendly conversation, Bengali style, as
patients waited for their daily treatment. A few yards away sat Dr. Ernest Muir,
an eminent doctor and a famous leprologist who had written one of the first
textbooks on leprosy. He was a tall, thin and seemingly dour Scotsman but he
had an impish sense of humour and a smile that lit up his face. He'd volunteered
to come back to India in his seventies to help out yet again. His third
incarnation, he joked.

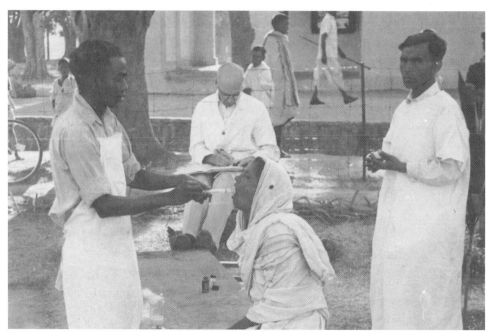

Dr Ernest Muir, seated, supervises early
experiments with DDS treatment, 1951

- 48 -

Each patient responded to his name, put his head back and opened his mouth. An assistant squirted in a small quantity of white liquid. It was a suspension of a newly-introduced drug, *diamino diphenyl sulphone* (DDS), dapsone. It had been synthesised by two German research workers in 1908 but little use was found for it. Some years later it was tried in large doses as a possible treatment for leprosy but it proved toxic and was shelved. Then, in 1941 it was tried in much smaller doses in the USA. Within months there were dramatic signs of improvement.

But there were problems. Some patients reacted badly even to the smaller doses given and suffered severe joint pain and fever. Dosage was cut down even more and still many patients continued to improve. Interest spread and in the late 1940s a few centres began tentative experiments with the drug. In Purulia Dr. Muir extended its use to 150 patients and most began to make progress. It was certainly more effective than any past medicine. The standard treatment at that time was regular injections of chaulmoogra oil, a painful process particularly for the children. And it didn't do much good. It was true that some patients got better while on it and that the tell-tale skin patches disappeared, but sometimes early leprosy can be self healing without treatment and the efficacy of chaulmoogra was debatable.

Before dapsone many patients coming into the centre expected to be there for most of their lives. Originally it was called Purulia Leprosy Asylum. An asylum is a place of refuge, a shelter. Then it changed to Purulia Leprosy Home and Hospital. The Hospital promised better quality care but the emphasis was still on the Home part. This was all set to change. There was a new feeling of hope in the air, created by the first results of this new medicine. The changes in individual patients were real, tangible, noticeable.

We were cautiously optimistic. In the past possible remedies had come - and gone. Hopes had been raised - and dashed. With the new treatment some patients became negative. That is, the microscope showed only dead bacilli in the skin although the debris took a long time to disappear. Even advanced cases improved although it took some months for noticeable change. The power of this new drug became undeniable. Research went on and as reports began to come in from a widening circle of leprosy workers in India, parts of Africa, and the USA, excitement increased. At first it was expensive and in short supply. Then production costs were cut and DDS was welcomed as the greatest advance in years. It was now given by a proper injection but as time passed this was replaced with tablets, much easier to administer, although many village patients still preferred the drama of injections.

In time the trickle of symptom-free patients grew. There was great rejoicing as they were presented with their certificates of health and discharged, usually with some public ceremony at the hospital. But the new hope brought new pressures. With a treatment that really worked more new patients were coming than ever before. However, experience with the new drug and its side effects was still limited and it could only be given safely to patients living in the centre.

Almost every day we were faced with desperate decisions. Under the banyan tree outside were always people waiting. Early cases, not yet disfigured or disabled. Old patients with hands damaged and useless, feet with infected ulcers covered in filthy rags. Men and women, some still capable of working, others fit

One of many hoping for admission, 1950s

only to beg. And then there were the children, often bone-thin, malnourished and neglected. We never refused to admit a child even when we were overcrowded but with the adults it was harder. There was never room for all.

We had to make heart-rending choices. Should we take in the old and helpless who needed compassionate care and shelter but who would be with us for life? If we did they'd prevent us from taking a succession of younger people who could be treated successfully and discharged. Or should we bypass the old and take in the younger to whom we could offer hope of a return to ordinary life? We couldn't always agree among ourselves. There were times when the doctors wanted to admit more and more people even though the place was bursting at the seams and our finite budget just wouldn't stand it. Telling sufferers that we didn't have the resources or the space to care for them didn't help. Even when we couldn't take them in we offered medical care before sending them away, but that wasn't always enough.

I felt moments of near despair. We all did. The tidal flow of suffering people was constant. It never ebbed. There were people squatting under the banyan tree every day of the week, begging for the shelter they needed. There were times when I would try to avoid them, to hide in my office and hope they'd be gone by the time I'd done my paperwork. The stark reality was that we could only offer shelter to a few. And if we couldn't help there was little chance that anyone else would.

The decision was often mine. A responsibility I didn't enjoy. The results could be hard to live with. I remember an elderly man, emaciated and weak, with ulcerated feet, begging to be taken in. We really had no room. We'd admitted other people that day and we had to draw the line. Behind him there were others. Take him in and I'd be faced with the same problem again with the next in line. I said no, sorry.

He wouldn't give in, he was desperate. Late in the afternoon he accepted the decision and went away. I breathed a sigh of relief and tried to forget him. The next morning we found he'd come back in the night and died under a tree behind my office. With the nurses I carried him to the mortuary but it did nothing to help him and little to comfort me. There were others, constant challenges both to our compassion and our finances. It was hard living with our failures.

As knowledge grew about dosage and the management of the new treatment, the pressure increased even more. We began to compare the possibilities of treatment with the realities of daily results. So much could now be done. Admit a patient in a relatively early stage of the illness and it could be controlled and deformity prevented. Yet how few people were benefiting. For every patient in the hospital there were hundreds outside. We began sending yet more people home so that others could be admitted in their places. Some didn't want to go. They'd been in the centre many years and were institutionalised. But others were glad to leave. One woman who'd spent several years with us took her certificate saying "My hands are all right, my feet are all right, my eyes and my mind are all right. Now I'm going home." But the homecoming often wasn't *all right*. Families frequently didn't want the old patients back; they couldn't cope with them.

For centuries leprosy had been incurable. It was hard to change beliefs and attitudes overnight in village India. Prejudice was strong. If a family was known to have a leprosy patient among them, even one with a certificate of health, their status was diminished. It would be hard for their sons to marry, almost impossible for their daughters. Sometimes it wasn't so much prejudice as poverty. And poverty was widespread and real. A family on the breadline found it tough to accept back a relative who'd been away for years, who would be another mouth to feed out of very limited resources, and who might not be fit to work. Some found the fight too hard and returned to us hoping we'd take them back. Others finished in Simonpur, the beggar village.

With other workers I spent days in the Land Rover bumping over rough village tracks to talk to and persuade families to care for their own relatives. It was hard going. One day we left early, shadows still long on the ground. Moving out of the town the road took us through dusty fields, their surface dry and cracked under the sun. It emphasised the harshness of life, the struggle to survive with only one rice crop each year. When the rains failed there was nothing. Then came a stretch of jungle. Not luxuriant growth, just a dense forest of low scrub and stunted, twisted trees. Leaves hung limp, brown and brittle, old warriors in rusted armour waiting to be carried off by the wind. Here and there, incredibly, a few fresh green leaves showed with an occasional patch of brilliant and defiant vermilion blossom from the *palash* trees.

After 20 miles we turned onto a cart track leading towards the hills. It deteriorated rapidly as it wound through an irresponsible tumble of rock, rough slopes and sudden gullies. From here on it was four-wheel drive. In the next ten miles we crossed five river beds of deep loose sand, banks eroded and ill-defined. We might have turned back if we'd known there were nine more to come. The jungle became wilder but every few miles we found a small village huddled in a patch of open fields. Our guide told us what he knew of each village. Pathardih had many stone-built houses. *Pathar* means stone in Bengali. The next village was known for the dolls and images of the gods made there in clay or papier mâché. Baghmundi actually boasted a police station and a dispensary with its own doctor.

As we reached its outskirts a giant *simul* tree rose straight and tall, silver bark brave against the blue sky. It had no leaves but clothing it with black foliage were hundreds of flying foxes, bats with bodies the size of large rats hanging upside down, asleep but in constant chittering restless movement. Also slung from the underside of several branches were white and chestnut coloured nests, three or four feet across, the homes of wild bees.

On another occasion bees disrupted one of our clinics. A patient walking through the forest had tried to get at their honey. They attacked him. Badly stung, he ran to the clinic for help but the bees came with him. They widened their attack to our workers, who took refuge in the Land Rover and sat huddled there for more than an hour. The clinic had to close for the day. The patients had left anyway. Hurriedly.

There were many people on the road. Men walked along, each with a stout stick or bow and arrows, or a long-handled axe carried over the shoulder. Weapons to promote courage on the long walk home at dusk. Women followed at the men's heels. No village woman walked alongside her husband. Almost all carried something. A basket of vegetables, a bundle of firewood, a baby, or a couple of live chickens, legs trussed, heads down, swinging from a pole. Some men cradled beautifully-coloured and pugnacious cockerels.

Cockfighting was a highly popular village sport. It was illegal but the local policeman often came to watch and gamble.

We came to Kareng, a bigger, slightly more prosperous village. We were looking for the home of Ronu, an elderly patient now symptom-free. He'd gone home once but come back, saying no one would accept him. A crowd of naked laughing children escorted us over fields to a group of small sorrowful huts in a glade of trees. The walls were crumbling, the thatch ragged and grey. One hut belonged to Ronu, another to his brother. Ronu's wife emerged as we arrived. She was old, wrinkled as a prune and almost the same

Beggars under banyan tree
Watercolour
1958

colour. She was desperately thin. She wore a threadbare off-white sari wrapped around her. Nothing else.

The brother appeared. He understood our Bengali better and was more articulate. Yes, they knew Ronu was now healthy, but if he came back how would he live? How could they keep him? What would he eat? They had no resources and only a tiny piece of land. They were old and weak. They had to employ a villager to farm their land, and he took half their crop as his share. In the worst times of the year they had to borrow from their neighbours, only marginally better off.

Other villagers joined us. No discussion is private in village India. They were friendly but concerned. It was obvious to all of us that an extra mouth to feed would soon reduce them to permanent begging. We accepted the facts and took him back. He was one patient we had to keep.

Purulia was the first leprosy centre in India to appoint a social worker to try to deal with this sort of problem although we didn't label him with that title. Pramod Kumar Roy was the son of a dedicated Indian Christian doctor who'd given a lifetime of service to leprosy sufferers. With a degree in history, he wasn't actually qualified for social work and had no experience, but trained ones were few and didn't want to get involved in leprosy work. We agreed with him that he'd be Welfare Officer. He was young, highly intelligent, committed and motivated. We learned together. He befriended the patients, gained their confidence, entered into their life stories and helped many. Today he is in Delhi, a senior executive of the Mission attached to its Southern Asia Office.

There were encouragements. Lal Mohan had been in the centre for several years. He was brought as a child and went through the school as far as he could go. He was a natural leader, tall, intelligent, quick. He had teenage clashes with authority, but he and authority survived. While under treatment he trained as a nurse-aide and began to mature. Beneath the banyan tree he was given his certificate of health and told he could go home. He was happy but apprehensive, unsure of his reception. His parents would welcome him but he wasn't so sure about the neighbours. "If I'm not allowed to stay can I come back?" he asked. I was non-committal.

He went home. Three days later he came back. Not on foot but on a borrowed bicycle. He'd come 30 miles in the heat to give us the news. His parents were grateful. This was good, but more encouraging was the attitude of others. The *gram panchayat*, the group of elders who manage village affairs, had accepted him. Now through him they were asking if we could take out the medicine that had made Lal Mohan better to treat other patients.

CHAPTER EIGHT

Expanding Horizons

However much we tried to increase our efforts pressure continued. There were still far too many people needing treatment and too few places available for them. We needed to move out. I covered one wall of my office with detailed ordnance survey maps of the whole area. We interviewed several hundred patients, including many of the now increasing number of outpatients who came, to find their homes on the map and build a picture of the main focuses of the illness.

There were interesting sidelights. A number of patients shuffled their feet in embarrassment as questioning showed that they'd given false addresses and even false names. They wanted to shield their families from identification, but we slowly built up a reasonably accurate picture which indicated where we should locate our first clinics to reach most sufferers.

We settled on Jhalda, a small town 28 miles away on a surfaced main road. That meant a ten-foot width of tarmac with wide tree-lined earth shoulders each side. Driving in India is a dangerous occupation and demands nerves of steel. The most important piece of equipment in an Indian vehicle is the horn rather than the brakes. Trucks seem to be driven by frustrated fighter pilots. They thunder towards you in the middle of the tarmac playing chicken. Both parties maintain their position until the very last moment before the smaller vehicle swerves to

The weekly market at Jhalda, near our clinic

the side. It doesn't always work, especially in the rains when the earth shoulders can turn into mud. The main roads are always littered with wrecked vehicles but it has little effect on other drivers.

One morning we drove to Jhalda after positive noises from local government. We cleared the way with two helpful meetings with the town's leaders who offered us a place to begin. It was a patch of land no-one else wanted and wasn't very

salubrious. It was on the edge of the weekly open air market. We chose market day for our weekly clinic so that patients could combine their visit to us with their shopping. Unfortunately the site was next to the open area where cattle were sold. On a busy market day there could be 200 cattle for sale and many big, black water buffalo, the air redolent with their presence. The smell attracted hordes of flies. From early in the morning there'd be streams of people coming to the market from all directions walking single file along the paths across the fields. Among them many *Santals*, tribal people, small and dark-skinned, the women splendid in heavy silver bangles and earrings, and in red-bordered hand-woven white saris.

We arrived for the first clinic. The flies abandoned the cows and water buffalo and hit us in swarms. It was a great start. For several weeks we'd publicised the clinic, mostly by word of mouth, both in Jhalda and through those of our outpatients who lived nearby. It would save them a 56-mile round trip if they used the clinic. It was September, in the middle of the rainy season and the rain poured down. There's nothing wetter than monsoon rain. We were soaked in seconds and the sudden drop in temperature that the downpour brought made us shiver. We had no idea how many patients would come and didn't really expect any in the rain. We opened the back of the Land Rover and waited. Our lack of faith reproached us. From a group of trees some yards away a small procession of black umbrellas emerged. They bobbed up and down as a dozen people hurried over. We were in business. For two and a half hours we worked steadily until finally 73 people had been registered and treated.

As we worked I remembered an old tent lying bundled in a store room at the centre. Later we used that, then progressed to a strong tarpaulin stretched from the side of the Land Rover. The fourth week 99 patients attended and as we packed up and were moving off a man waved frantically. He was late, he'd been delayed. We stopped, gave him his medicine and chalked up our first century.

In time we moved a little further away from the cattle market to the slope of a nearby hillock and it was here that we sited our first village clinic almost a year later. It was bare and stony but looked out across the valley to green hills. It caught whatever breeze there was and, more importantly, most of the flies stayed at the cattle market, although the same couldn't be said for the mosquitoes.

We called a gang of village workmen to build the mud-walled clinic towards the end of the next hot weather. We measured out the foundations with bamboo

Near the site of our first outpatient clinic at Jhalda

stakes as markers. The men squatted on their haunches and lit their *biris*, locally-made cigarettes which are just a pinch of strong tobacco wrapped in a leaf from a tree. Their faces were blank.

"Well," I asked. "How much?"

"It's a big building," said the spokesman, looking into the distance.

"Not as big as all that," I countered.

"There's not much time before the rains," he complained.

"The quicker you work, the greater your daily rate," I said. "How much?" He shifted his weight from one leg to the other, looked benevolently at an ant crawling near his big toe and suggested a highly inflated figure. We laughed politely and he looked slightly affronted. We said he had a great sense of humour and assured him we hadn't been born yesterday.

"How much do you offer?" he asked without the slightest sign of interest. We named a figure well on the low side. His eyes widened in simulated shock. He told us how poor they all were, how large their families and how the price of rice had increased. Did we want them to starve? Speed was out of the question. Both sides had to be satisfied. Eventually a price was agreed. They did a good job. The building lasted years until we replaced it with a brick-built cottage hospital with staff quarters for paramedical workers who used it as their base for more sophisticated survey and control work throughout the area.

We looked for our next site at Jeypur, halfway between Jhalda and Purulia. On first acquaintance the Raja of Jeypur didn't match the image the title conjures up. No impression of wealth or splendour, but he owned most of the land in the area. His house was set well back from the main road in a big, bare compound. It was an imposing two-storeyed building – or it would have been if it had ever been finished. As it was it remained a memorial to unfulfilled ambition. The ground floor was habitable but the upper storey had never been roofed nor plastered, and crumbling red brick offered a toehold to grass and weeds. Marks of rain stained the walls like dried tears. To one side was a mud-walled, thatched cattle shed and inside the Raja's ancient red and cream Citroen car. A chicken perched on its roof.

There were no peacock feathers to this Raja, no satin or jewels. He was in late middle age, slightly above average height and sturdy. His face was broad and fair, with pale piercing eyes that looked directly at me. He had long greying hair down to his shoulders. He wore a half-sleeved vest, a *dhoti* (a plain cloth folded and pleated to cover his legs), an unbleached cotton shawl and a sacred thread, signifying him as a twice-born upper caste Hindu. He was barefoot. Devout in his own faith, he was helpful and concerned for his people. After friendly negotiation he gave us a patch of flat land set among twisted *palash* trees just off the main road and here we built our second clinic.

The clinics attracted many new patients but we soon realised that these were only part of the answer. We had to move even closer to our patients. We were only getting those with the courage, initiative and strength to take the first step and come to us. There were many more still without help, vainly hiding their illness until they couldn't hide it any longer.

In 1960 we sent out our first paramedical workers to live at Jhalda and work from there out into the villages. They began house-to-house surveys examining almost all the population. They gave simple health talks and at opportune times and places opened up new clinics. Sometimes these were in small buildings, often what we came to call mango tree clinics because they simply met under the shade by the road side. From these beginnings grew one of the early SET – Survey, Education and Treatment – leprosy control programmes and before long patients were numbered in thousands rather than hundreds.

Gradually the clinics took some of the pressure from the centre although admissions to the acute beds in the hospital wards had to be reorganised. With so many more patients under treatment, an increasing number needed bed care for a limited time for painful episodes of reaction and the early treatment of foot ulcers.

Other leprosy centres in India began to face the challenge of change. Workers began to come to Purulia to see what we were doing. We made no pretence that it was perfect but it was bringing patients out of hiding. Before long we began to organise training programmes for paramedical workers and, later, physiotherapy technicians. We cooperated with the *Hind Kusth Nivaran Sangh* – literally The Indian Society for the Eradication of Leprosy – a national voluntary agency, and designed courses which led to government recognised certificates. There were also courses for doctors. Then training for shoe and artificial limb makers. Leprosy was on the move.

We were facing great changes in India. In the late 1950s and early 1960s people were shrugging off the legacy of the British Raj and exercising their new freedom. It wasn't always easy, living with a foot in each camp. We were English but had never known the Raj, and our sympathies were all with independent India. But we were also Christian and some saw the Christian church and its work as part of the old colonial package. We faced questions. Criticism of Christian activity came from two sides, from right-wing Hindu movements and from left-wing politicians. Leprosy hospitals were not immune in spite of the humanitarian work they did.

We went on home leave in 1962 and Bill Bailey, the Mission's Field Secretary, took over the hospital responsibility from me. A few patients in the leprosy hospital were discontented. Stirred up by outside anti-Christian agitators they made impossible demands and organised a strike. It turned ugly. Bill was normally a superb manager but he broke down under the strain and was flown home. I said I was willing to return if I could continue my English home leave later. We needed it after five years in India but the Mission put in another interim manager.

The situation came to a head over something as seemingly trivial as the sweeping of an open drain. The strikers refused to do it. The English doctor and nursing sister decided that if no one else would they'd do it themselves. The strikers saw this as provocation. The doctor and nurse were beaten up and, although not seriously injured, the police were called. The strike was called off.

We returned to a very uneasy peace. The atmosphere of trust and goodwill built up over the years was damaged but with patience and the slow build-up of a new understanding, the place gradually returned to normal. Within the next two and a half years I was asked to advise and deal with similar situations in three other Indian leprosy hospitals. It was a learning process for all of us. While there were certainly agitators at work around these centres, I don't believe they were solely to blame.

Management in many Christian centres was paternal and centralised. Patients were "done good to". They were expected to do what they were told and not to question what was being done to help them. I suspect the minor violence we sometimes encountered arose more from frustration than evil intent. I didn't always appreciate it at the time but the fact that patients were now questioning what we did was a measure of success. People browbeaten by prejudice and illness were exerting their own rights and grasping at dignity.

We were slow at first to understand and welcome these changes but we rejoice in the progress made recently. Over the last few years patients' voices have been heard and listened to increasingly. Today they're seen not so much as mute recipients of well-meaning charity but as partners in a joint enterprise. We can learn from each other.

There were other communal strains in India. Hindu and Muslim didn't always find it easy to live with each other and whenever tension rose between India and Pakistan, it created local problems too. On one occasion communal riots began in the north and spread through much of the country. There was killing in Calcutta. The violence got nearer. Muslims were killed in Purulia town. We had a small group of Muslim patients and, although we'd never had any overt communal trouble in the hospital, I made sure I knew where they were located and kept a watchful eye on them. I had plans to move them down to the staff quarters if they seemed to be in danger, but felt that to act prematurely might bring on the violence I hoped we could prevent. Life was tense.

One afternoon I walked through the hospital grounds. Under a tree I saw a small huddle of patients. It worried me. I approached them slowly, casually. One was reading out aloud from a newspaper. It described the riots, the killings. They shook their heads in disbelief. "It's terrible," they said. I looked at the group. Among them were all three faiths, Hindu, Muslim, Christian. There was no animosity between them. It was as though it was all happening in a different country. We talked together about the violence and all condemned it. Sometimes leprosy can unite people in a positive way. Our patients shared a common suffering and had felt the same sense of rejection. We had no trouble.

Bengal village
Watercolour
1962

CHAPTER NINE
Into Bhutan

Stones were still bouncing down as we drove round a corner in the mist. An avalanche. It left a raw wound on the face of the hillside biting down to the underlying rocks. The soil was loose and shifting. A trickle of water added to the instability. It seeped round the stones, undermining, loosening. As we watched another rock crashed onto the pile of earth and boulders blocking the road. Some were the size of a man and they piled up in heavy heaps where the road had been. Road is a misnomer. It was just a rough track gouged out of the mountainside by the bulldozers Indian Army engineers were using to build the first road into Bhutan. The avalanche was a hundred yards wide, the end hidden in the mist which swirled and deepened in the evening twilight.

A few men appeared at the far end of the fall and began clambering over the rocks, barefoot and agile, watching all the time for danger from above. Their voices echoed and more men appeared with crowbars. A few of the smaller stones were heaved over the edge to crash down the slope for hundreds of feet and shatter on the rock face below, but darkness soon stopped the clearing work. We were stuck and needed shelter for the night.

There were four of us. Dr. Victor Das, The Leprosy Mission's Secretary for Southern Asia, 'Farmer Chandy', an Indian doctor grown old and experienced in the Mission's service, the driver of the overloaded jeep, and myself. We were responding to an invitation from the Government of Bhutan to look at the leprosy situation. Not to begin work but to explore. To learn something of conditions in the country, to assess the need, to find out if there was anything the Mission could do to help. It was September 1964.

The road workers invited us to share their shack a hundred yards back along the road. Four walls and a roof of lopped tree branches and interwoven leaves perched on a flat square of ground above the road. We shared it with 16 Nepali labourers, full of friendliness and courtesy. They gave us beds rough-cut from thin branches and padded with ferns and leaves. We opened a couple of cans of baked beans and a tin of fruit and bedded down as soon as we had eaten. We slept just below a layer of smoke which spread lazily from cooking fires at one end of the hut. The smoke hung, gently turning and billowing, inches above our faces. The night was quiet, a silence heightened by the dull roar of a torrent deep down in the valley fed by the rain which had caused the rock fall.

The road, now blocked, stretched 120 miles into Bhutan, from its southern border with India to the Bhutanese capital, Thimpu. It had taken two years to hack out the rough track through the Eastern Himalayas sufficiently for four-wheel drive vehicles to make the journey. It took 48 hours when things went right. Before the road was built it was at least a six-day trek through leech-thick jungle over muscle-stretching mountain paths.

As though the road wasn't a sufficient barrier, a strict control was kept on the number of foreigners entering the country. Like Tibet and Nepal, Bhutan had closed its doors, pulled up its drawbridges and lived in feudal isolation for generations. Geography had helped. Sandwiched between India and Tibet, Bhutan is mountainous. The road from India ran in from the border through a few miles of flat forest, then rose and heaved itself over the foothills. The lower slopes were covered in mossy trees and thickets of rhododendron. The way writhed and twisted over the mountains, higher and higher, teetering over 9,000 feet high passes, an insignificant scratch on the surface of the land. It then petered out at Thimpu but mule tracks led further north, pushing up to the snow line and beyond, to the Great Himalayas of the northern frontier with Tibet, 24,000 feet above sea level.

Bhutan journey, 1964/5

Occasionally a missionary had been allowed over the border but only one had penetrated far or stayed long. He was Dr. Gordon Craig, for many years in charge of the leprosy home at Kalimpong in the north of West Bengal. Some Bhutanese leprosy sufferers had gone there for treatment over the years and Craig was invited into Bhutan by the late king. Missionary work though was forbidden in a country which was then, and still is now, powerfully Buddhist.

The mist still curtained the hills as we awoke. Smells of acrid tobacco fumes greeted us and a dawn chorus of hacking coughs but, with more men on the road and the welcome arrival of a bulldozer, a rough track was cleared within three hours. The jeep moved slowly over the shifting earth, hugging the mountainside, although I took the precaution of walking across the unstable cutting after the jeep.

As we neared our destination the road divided, one branch going east to Thimpu, the other continuing up the Paro valley. The valley begins as a narrow gorge, confining the Paro river, which froths and roars as it leaps along its rocky bed. Ice cold, the water drains directly from the glaciers to the north. A mile further on and the valley broadens out but never to more than a mile or so wide.

The valley floor is more than 7,000 feet above sea level, the surrounding mountains much higher. Houses appear in groups of two or three, family settlements surrounded by terraced fields of millet and rice. Wide banks of pink cosmos flower wild on bare hillsides.

The houses are solid, heavy wooden frames supporting rammed earth walls. Roofs are made of rough planks split from logs and laid two or three layers deep. They are anchored by their own weight and by strategically placed stones picked from the river bed. The ground floor shelters the animals, cows, goats and horses, their heat in winter helping to keep warm the humans who live on the floor immediately above them. The open lofts above are stacked with straw and the roofs are often vivid carpets of hot red chillies drying in the sun.

The family lives in one or two large rooms, sparse and dark, lit by small latticed windows without glass, but wooden shuttered. Cooking fires in the corner add smoke and soot. There are thin mattresses on the wooden floor, a low carved table, a few chests. Pots and pans, bows and arrows, swords in beautifully-patterned silver scabbards, and old baskets hang from the walls in the gloom. One corner is partitioned off as the prayer room. The room flickers with the smoky glow of butter oil lamps burning on the family altar. Behind them gleams the small golden image of the Buddha, cross-legged, hands folded in meditation, face serene and detached.

The people are warm and friendly. High cheek-boned, rosy skins fair but weather-worn by sun and wind, they are a robust hill people, tough and hardy but quick to smile. For many mine was the first European face they'd seen, but curiosity was tempered with a gentle courtesy. Yet this wasn't an idyllic landscape of happy simple people. No Shangri-la. Life could be tough, was tough. There was disease: goitre, through lack of iodine in the diet, tapeworm, hookworm, dysentery, tuberculosis and leprosy. Many children died in infancy.

We arrived at the government guest house in Paro, sore, aching and weary. It was built high on a hillside, looking out over the fields below. Rice was ripening, patches of bright green and gold, ochre and brown. Narrow irrigation channels stitched silver threads across the fields. Long lines of prayer flags marched through the crops. Prayers were printed from hand-carved wood blocks onto lengths of coarse white cloth. These were attached to tall bamboos and as the wind flapped the flags, the prayers scattered blessings on the land.

Beyond the fields the four-tiered pagoda of the royal guest house nestled within three walled courtyards, one inside the other. Dragons and lotus flowers carved in relief and painted in strident primary colours vibrated over the building which lay at the end of a narrow road through a delicacy of willow trees. Above, on the far hillside was the *dzong*, white and solid, window openings set high in the walls. It was a walled city in itself. A great complex of monastery, Buddhist temple, fort and government offices. It stood solid and strong inside rings of parapet walls which had protected it in the past from the attacks of rival war lords.

We were shown round the temple later by a *lama*, a shaven-headed monk robed in shades of purple and magenta. We climbed ladders from floor to floor, up to the sanctuary where the main image of the Buddha reigns. Its golden form, 15 feet high, rested in shadow half obscured by heavy tapestries and the smoky miasma of incense and butter oil lamps. The walls were covered by *thankas*, religious paintings framed in many-coloured silks. Larger wall paintings showed awesome saints and demons. There were carved masks, military style uniforms from times long gone, swords, drums, long horns.

A few days later, higher up the valley and within 30 miles of the Tibetan border where jagged teeth of rock tear the clouds to shreds we visited a smaller temple. We talked to the *lama*. "Yes," he said, "there are people in the valley with leprosy. They come to the temple to pray and make offerings, but it does little good." He shrugged. "What they really need is the medicine we've heard about, but which only the rich can get by travelling to India."

We met a Tibetan refugee who, like many others, had lived in Bhutan since escaping from Chinese Communist rule in his own country. He took us up the valley for another mile to the home of one patient. She was about 45 years old. She limped out of her house on badly damaged feet, her hands almost fingerless. Her face had all the marks of old, untreated leprosy. The heavy wrinkles, the lopsided quizzical look that nerve damage and paralysis leave, the lack of sparkle in the eyes, the resigned dull look of long years of pain endured without hope. The wreckage of life that we've seen so often.

She told us of other sufferers who lived on the other side of the icy, green, glacial river that flowed just beyond the boundary of her garden. In the shadow of the *dzong*

Untreated leprosy patient in Bhutan
1964

we found a small wooden building, a dispensary where an Indian doctor was working for the government on a short term contract. He'd seen leprosy sufferers but knew little about treating the disease. There were, at that time, in the whole of Bhutan only a dozen doctors for perhaps a million people scattered throughout a country the size of Switzerland.

We talked with the Prime Minister, H.E.Lendrup Dorji, and other officials. The meetings were refreshingly informal. Later he took us to fish for trout in the cold glacial river. Around the edges of our party there were guards armed with modern automatic weapons. He was taking no chances. His predecessor, who had originally invited the Mission to visit Bhutan, had been assassinated a year before by a reactionary group of people who opposed opening up the country to outside influence.

We moved on to Thimpu, the capital, a wide conglomerate of mostly single storied buildings in a valley sheltered on all four sides by high mountain walls. Like Paro, it too was powerfully overshadowed by an enormous *dzong*. Nearby was a whole ocean of white prayer flags, flapping perpetually like restless sea birds. It marked the place where the late prime minister had been cremated a year before. There was a clean and well run 70-bed government hospital in Thimpu, run by an able young Bhutanese doctor, although with limited equipment. He had little trained help but was doing all he could.

There were leprosy sufferers here too. One a quiet, bewildered boy of 14, face swollen, eyebrows destroyed. He had been brought by his father from a remote valley 20 days trek from the town. But there was no treatment for him.

It was hard to face such suffering with empty hands. We could offer no immediate help, no hope. We couldn't even promise that we'd come back. Decisions hadn't yet been made. By this time, Barbara and I had two daughters, Stephanie and Jennifer. I thought of them, both born healthy in India, and now at a good school with medical care available so easily when they needed it. Blessings we took for granted.

We walked through the weekly market and were objects of gentle interest. People had hiked in from distant hamlets carrying on their backs the produce they had for sale. Fruit and vegetables, hand-woven cloth, freshly-butchered pigs, live chickens. There were itinerant travellers too with small goods from India – torches and batteries, safety pins, and exotic new toys like ball-point pens. All laid out on the open ground, in woven baskets, on small squares of once-white cloth.

It was an endlessly shifting crowd of colour and noise and argument, laughing, shouting, bargaining, protesting. A mix of Tibetans and Nepalese as well as Bhutanese. We pushed through and were led out of the bazaar to a small house. We jumped a stagnant drain, walked a plank over a pool of mud and ducked through the low door.

Through the darkness came the thud of weaving. Two women sat on the floor working simple looms, creating with great patience and labour the precious cloth which is the basis of Bhutan's traditional costume. One woman showed us her back with a raised tell-tale patch of early leprosy. Her baby suckled placidly, oblivious to the stress around her. "There is so little we can do for them," our guide told us.

The situation cried out for help without delay. Too many lives were being damaged and destroyed by suffering we could prevent. We had to put in a strong and positive report. The Mission had always been able to find the resources when challenged by tragedy like this, and had to do so now.

Our determination was made even stronger as we began the hard jeep journey back through the mountains to India. As we drove along in the morning sunshine we pulled aside from time to time to allow mule trains to pass, the animals labouring up the hills under heavy packs. We could usually hear them coming before we saw them, the brass bells hung around the necks of the lead mules echoing above the sound of the jeep engine. As they went by flashes of light reflected from the mirror on the first mule's forehead, there to ward off evil spirits. Alongside them the muleteers walked in their heavy felt boots with a loose easy stride that seemed to make light of both altitude and distance.

We rounded a bend and a small family group moved to the road's edge to let us pass. Just a man and woman, each laden with a large backpack, and a dog. As we passed the man glanced up. What we saw in that brief moment made us stop and get out of the vehicle. His face was swollen and thickened, his eyes bright with fever. His fingers too were swollen, all signs that he had leprosy and was in a painful episode of reaction. He should have been in a hospital bed. Instead he was walking with a heavy pack to his home in Ha Valley, several days' journey away. Our minds were made up.

Back in Purulia I wrote our report for the International Office of the Mission in London, recommending that work begin. Questions were asked. The Government of Bhutan valued the work we could do but they also recognised our Christian motivation. They welcomed our medical work but said very firmly that evangelism and any overt Christian witness would not be allowed. Should we accept such restrictions?

My answer was a strong yes. If our motivation and beliefs didn't communicate themselves through our lives and daily work then words wouldn't help much. And to deny the medical and compassionate care we could give to sufferers themselves because of some restrictions on our activities didn't seem to me to be living out the Christian gospel. We are called to help people in need whatever the cost. There were some outside the Mission who were critical of our stance, but then there always are. We knew we were doing the right thing.

Within a few months the first Leprosy Mission doctor had volunteered to begin work there. He was Gottfried Riedel, an experienced German doctor who had joined TLM in 1951, the first German to join us after the end of World War Two. He and his wife Helle did a magnificent pioneering job and were followed by many others from the United Kingdom, Finland and elsewhere.

Over the years that followed the Mission gradually built up and expanded its work until we were responsible for leprosy control over the whole country. The work was based on five hospitals, built jointly by the Mission and the Bhutanese Government. Over the next 30 years leprosy was brought under control and, as I write, TLM is in the process of handing over all its work to the government, the need for our presence almost over. We leave behind a tradition of honest, faithful service and many lives saved from illness and tragedy.

From the beginning TLM's work in Bhutan has been an integrated service, open to all who are sick, not just leprosy sufferers. It had to be, there was so little medical care available in the early days. It would have been impossible to treat leprosy sufferers and turn away others who needed medical help.

On one visit I did a two-day trek with a doctor and nurse, porters and ponies. We set off at dawn as the sun began to warm the freezing air. For two hours we followed the river, gradually gaining height. Then the real climb began through golden grass and superb pine trees. The path was steep and rough. Life soon focused on the next step, the next breath and the sweat. We arrived at Chamang mid-afternoon after six hours' walking. It was a small hamlet and we pitched our tent near the home of the *gapo*, the local headman. We struggled into our sleeping bags early and were soon asleep.

Medical work began the next morning at six o'clock. There was frost on the ground so we set up the clinic in a room in the *gapo's* house. Patients arrived all morning. Some with trivial complaints, others with severe problems. For some we were too late. Twenty children had died of whooping cough a few weeks earlier. Limited surveys gave an infant mortality rate of almost 50 per cent. Half the children born alive would die before they were five years old, many of them from preventable illness.

After the clinic which lasted all morning, Reino Aalho, the doctor, went round a few of the houses to check on patients he'd seen on a visit a month earlier. One was a pale, thin woman in her twenties. She had tuberculosis. Reino was pleased with her progress. "If she goes on like this," he said, "she'll soon be strong enough to make the trek to the hospital." In Bhutan you had to be strong to travel for medical care. A catch-22 situation.

During one of several later journeys in Bhutan Barbara and I arrived in Mongar, a major town in the east of the country, in time for *Tche Tchu*. It's an annual festival to celebrate the founding of the *dzong*, a sort of church anniversary. But it's an anniversary with a difference. People trek in for miles around. The large open courtyard at the centre of the *dzong* is decorated. A great religious painting, 30 feet high, 20 feet long, is hung from the upper floor windows down to ground level. Around the edges of the courtyard the crowd stands, several hundred people crushed together, children pushed to the front.

Monks dress in their finest and play out a rhythm with drums, cymbals and ten-foot-long horns. The sound echoes through the valley, a prelude to the dances. Other monks dress in traditional dance costumes, bright in coloured silks. They wear masks carved from wood, graphic depictions of saints and demons. The sound and vision is compelling. The dancers gyrate, faster and faster, the skirts of their costumes flaring out as

Bhutan, the dzong *at Tongsa*

they move. The drama builds, the tension lightened by the antics of a clown, his role and earthy humour greatly appreciated by the crowd. The celebration lasts several days, a time of colour and excitement.

From Mongar I walked to Lhuntse with Joyce Missing, one of TLM's most experienced workers. Lhuntse was a day's journey along a beautiful valley. Towards the end of the day we saw the *dzong* in the distance perched on a hill top and silhouetted against the darkening sky. There was a deep gorge to cross, spanned by a long suspension bridge. Three steel cables and a floor of wooden planks just wide enough to walk over. I asked to go first. I wanted to get some photographs of the others crossing with the ponies. There were smiles as I began to cross, holding on to the cables as the bridge began to sway. Looking down wasn't a good idea.

Safely over I set my cameras and signalled to the others to cross. Then there were more smiles. I asked what the joke was. "Well," they said, "we're never quite sure these bridges are safe so we usually send a pony across first." At Lhuntse the Mission developed a small cottage hospital with a wide outreach into areas that had never known good medical treatment.

Life could be hard for people living remote from health centres. Barbara and I made one journey over the lateral road that links the east and west of the country. The fact that the mountain ridges go north to south doesn't help. The road was a rough switchback, the highest pass more than 12,000 feet above sea level.

We spent a bitterly cold night in a rest house and in the morning the ground was thick with snow and ice and blanketed in a freezing mist. The driver of the Land Rover lit a small fire under the fuel tank to melt the diesel before he could start the engine. The journey took two long days. It was enlivened on the second day when we overturned at dusk. At a lower altitude the ice had turned to mud and on a particularly tricky bit of road we skidded. The road was narrow, there was no room to manoeuvre, the vehicle lost grip and over we went. Fortunately we slithered into the mountain side. The other side of the road was a drop of several hundred feet. After a moment's stunned silence we struggled out and ended the day with a walk of three or four miles slipping and sliding along a narrow trail in the dark, a little shaken but unharmed.

By next morning the vehicle had been rescued. We checked the chassis, steering, springs and brakes and resumed the journey. On the way we were asked to pick up a young woman, pregnant with her first baby and in deep trouble. She'd been in labour for two days already and was in great pain. She now had to endure a full day's bumping on the road before we reached the hospital at Thimpu. By then she was weak and unresponsive and we wondered what the outcome would be. The next morning we enquired. Everything was fine. The baby boy had been in a breech position but the bumping of the journey had turned it and he was born naturally soon after our arrival.

The journey was brought to a great conclusion when we were invited to lunch with His Majesty King Jigme Singje Wangchuk and the Queen Mother of Bhutan Ashi Keshang. We met in the grounds of the Detchencholing palace in a beautiful marquee of hand-painted silk. The ground around us had been covered in freshly-cut, aromatic pine branches. After the ceremonial and traditional exchange of white silk scarves and presents the party became very friendly and informal. Our lunch was served on silver plates, a meal of brown rice, yak meat and curried pheasant. We were surprised when the Queen Mother mentioned the accident we'd had on the road and asked if we'd recovered. Although the road was bad, modern radio communication was good and our progress across the country had been monitored.

Above, going to worship, Bhutan
Below, Buddist monks
Watercolour sketches

CHAPTER TEN
The India I Love

It's a November morning in the cold
weather in Purulia. It should really be called cooler weather as the temperature
never drops below about 50°F and midday is like a pleasant English summer day.
Dawn is uncompromising. Sky meets horizon sharp and clear. There are no
blurred edges. The bare dusty fields are resting after the effort of producing their
one crop of rice a year. There's no wind and over the distant village the blue-
grey smoke of kitchen fires floats. It rolls gently on itself, hardly moving. A herd
of bony cattle wanders slowly across the fields, grazing hopefully on the rapidly
diminishing grass left over from the rains. Sound carries, even the protesting
grunts and rumble of the animals.

Gently, tentatively at first but with a growing confidence there comes the
sound of a flute. The player sits hidden behind a tree, watching the animals. The
melody is soft, it hangs on the air by its fingertips. Liquid notes flow, ripple, fall
and twist in the morning air like a prayer. Its undemanding beauty offers itself
freely, in tune with the morning.

Another sound intrudes. An early bullock cart off to market. Iron-rimmed
wooden wheels screech a protest against the axle. The driver sits huddled at the
front of the cart, his head and shoulders shawl-wrapped against the cool air.
Then a sudden flapping of black wings as a group of crows caws its way into
the air. Another day has begun.

Dusk, too, leaves images in my mind. Dusk is called *godhuli*, the time of cow
dust. The cattle are going home, subdued after a day's foraging. They walk
quietly now, heads lowered, the only noise the scuffing of hooves on the earth.
Sunlight, gold and pink, slants almost horizontally through the trees that line the
road, now bright in light, now shadowed. A cloud of dust moves with the
animals, hovering around and above, picked out in brush strokes of brightness.

The sun itself, blood red and large, hesitates on the horizon, reluctant to leave,
then dips and disappears. There's an immediate chill. Colours fade, darken, and
the cattle in little groups each turn into the family courtyard. The young
cowherd slaps the last one on its rump, waves his stick and disappears.

Night brings a different beauty. There are few street lamps in village India and,
in our day, little electricity. The sky is huge, infinite, a great rich blackness with
stars so bright and near they almost join the family. When the moon rises it
lights the landscape in silver, bright enough to read by, for a few sentences
anyway. Stand still and you hear little noises. A rustling in the trees as flying
foxes stir and stretch. Smaller, unidentifiable sounds in the drying leaves on the
ground. Then suddenly the bark and howl of jackals, high-pitched and stark in
their intensity. A few short bursts of challenge to the moon and then they're
gone, leaving an empty space in the darkness. A couple of minutes go by and
the sound comes again, but from a different direction as they move on.

There's the simple, gracious hospitality of village folk. Rough and rutted tracks between the fields lead to villages that rarely see a car. Roads are hewn deep below the level of the fields by centuries of bullock carts. There are occasional wayside shrines, stones rough-carved with the image of *Ganesh* or *Hanuman*, smeared with red paste, a garland of withered marigolds draped around it. The Land Rover jolts its way along, no faster than the carts, springs creaking arthritically. There is a reserved curiosity among the adults as we arrive, less restrained among the children. This visit is a novelty for them. They call and run and stand around wide-eyed, absorbing every detail of the event. One toddler, overwhelmed, cries at the strangers and runs for safety to its mother. Laughter is shared.

Asking permission, we leave our shoes at the door of the house and stoop to enter. Wood is expensive and door frames are low. The host unrolls a mat and we're asked to sit. He squats opposite to entertain us. There is little furniture. A wooden-framed string bed with a hard pillow on it, a small rickety table, a few boxes, a stool and clothes hanging from lines stretched across a corner of the room. A whiff of blue smoke from the veranda, a sudden acrid smell as dried cow dung cakes smoulder into flame, the sound of water poured into an aluminium kettle. Tea is on its way.

It can be a long time coming, but that gives time for conversation. We talk briefly about the weather, then the harvest and the price of rice. Then the family, in detail. It's hard to identify each person, every relationship has a special name. Mother's first uncle's oldest son isn't easy to grasp. The tea arrives. It's robust. Tea leaves, sugar and milk are boiled and simmered together in the kettle. Sweet beyond imagining and often laced with root ginger and spices. Tea as you've never known it – less a drink, more an adventure.

Glass tumblers are placed before us on the earth floor. The tea is poured straight from the kettle. The tumbler fills and fills. The liquid hesitates at the rim, builds up and overflows. It slides down the glass and collects in a little pool around it. At first I wondered why it was done that way until I recognised the unspoken message. This was village hospitality. They might be poor but hospitality has no limits. No hostess would leave a grudging half inch of unfilled tumbler, she makes my cup full and running over. This was mirrored in the way wealthier people gave occasional gifts to the hospital. No one ever gave 50 or 100 or 1,000 rupees. It was always 51, 101, 1,001. The little extra every time.

As often as we could find excuse we called for Saturday picnics with the healthy children we cared for. We sat outside, cross-legged on the ground, banana leaf plates washed and still wet in front of us. We ate with our fingers. It was always the same menu. Unmilled rice, rough and red, its vitamins intact, boiled and heaped generously. *Dal*, a thick yellow lentil sauce. Goat curry, richly spiced and succulent from long simmering, its gravy rimmed in golden *ghee*. It shared space with a drier vegetable curry and always a little heap of coarse salt. At the end a sweet red chutney, still warm, cooked from fresh tomatoes and molasses. And if we were very lucky there'd be one of Bengal's prized sweetmeats. It might be *rasagula*, made from milk simmered to solid, shaped into balls and soaked in rose-water syrup. Nothing is sweeter. Or sometimes it was *sandesh*, like fudge but laced with pistachio.

There was always laughter at the meals and well-rehearsed jokes told each time with greater relish. The girls would pile our plates high and return challenging us to eat more. The only remedy a long Saturday afternoon sleep.

The greatest thrill was watching people change under care. Sukhni was one of many. She was about eight years old, she didn't know for sure. We found her under a tree one morning, alone. She was filthy, hair matted, her clothes just tattered rags. Her face was swollen in reaction to her leprosy, her eyes red-rimmed. Dirty bandages hid her feet. It was better not to stand downwind of her. Her hands too were swollen, irretrievably damaged by neglected infection and blistered by burns she hadn't felt. She was defensive and wary and kept a little distance between herself and anyone who spoke to her.

Eight-year-old Sukhni, just admitted for care, 1960

We took her in. She was cleaned up, freshly bandaged and clothed and given time to adjust. With care and regular food she was transformed. She brightened, shared her name and history with us. Later she smiled. As weeks turned into months she showed a growing confidence, suspicion gone. She joined the school, played as children should play, a future opening up. It didn't always happen this way, the happy endings could never be guaranteed but they made a welcome counterweight of encouragement to balance off the tragedies, the times we couldn't help.

Sharing in the regular communion services in the Church of the Good Samaritan was always a moving experience. Here we were all equal, patients and staff, the fit and the disabled. Most walked up to the rail and knelt. Some hobbled, clutching bamboo walking sticks. Others came on crutches or shuffled painfully along the ground. Shanti Babu, our minister, would always take the bread and wine to those who couldn't move, but most wanted to make the effort for themselves.

As he moved down the row hands were held out for the bread. Many were clawed or damaged by neglected leprosy. Some had little more than stumps. For these Shanti would gently push their heads back and put the bread straight into their mouths. Sometimes he'd dip the bread in the wine to avoid the problem of hands unable to grasp the common cup. There was healing in the moment. Not of the body but in a mystical sharing in Christ's suffering. Hardly recognised by some, but for others it brought a deep acceptance and joy.

Noonday sun, Purulia
Watercolour
1964

CHAPTER ELEVEN

African Journeys

Our daughters, Stephanie and Jenny, were growing up. They were happy at their boarding school in Darjeeling, but Barbara and I knew that the time was coming when we should go home. We needed to be a permanent family together and they needed the opportunity of fitting into their own culture. But it was tough on them. They didn't want to go. One day we told them we were going home. "But we are home," they responded. Purulia was home, India was the country in which they'd been born, grown up and gone to school. It was the country where all their friends lived. England was just somewhere they visited once every few years for a holiday and to meet grandparents they hardly knew.

There was another problem. I didn't want to go back to teaching. Experience in India had widened my horizons but I didn't know what came next. At this point Wilfrid Russell, the Mission's General Secretary, visited Purulia. We shared our concern with him. He smiled, inappropriately we thought. Then he said that one of the things he'd come to do was to offer me a new job in the International Office in London, but that folk there didn't know whether we'd be willing to uproot ourselves from India to take it. It didn't take us long to agree.

We left in 1965. It was traumatic and sad. We were leaving behind an enormous family into which we'd grown. Over the years we'd been accepted as part of the community in the centre and beyond it. We had friends, not only among the patients and staff, but also amongst the local townsfolk, Hindu as well as Christian. We were going to miss them. Wherever we travelled in India we felt welcomed. In city and village Indians have a great capacity for hospitality. Visitors are guests who are honoured.

As we were settling as a family into our new home in Ealing, I was finding my way through the workings of the International Office from which the worldwide activities of the Mission were co-ordinated. Far from being the desk job I'd thought it might be, within a few weeks I was asked to fly to Ethiopia to assess the possibilities of a new project. It was November 1965.

It was my first visit to Africa, apart from shopping in Port Said and visiting the pyramids in Egypt. It was exciting, my first experience of a continent very different from Asia. Ethiopia had a great leprosy problem. A conservative estimate put the number of sufferers at about 260,000 and only about 30,000 got any sort of treatment. Most people with leprosy could expect no more than uncontrolled illness, progressive deformity and acute social prejudice. Many lost their homes and land and finished as beggars. To be a beggar in one of the world's poorest countries is no joke.

Addis Ababa, with its comparative wealth and the tradition of alms-giving in the Ethiopian Orthodox Church, attracted many of these beggars. The government was trying to do something about it, although their answer seemed to be to push the problem away by moving the beggars out of town rather than tackling the underlying issues of poverty and illness. To be fair the country had many problems and few resources. The Health Ministry had set up a couple of agricultural rehabilitation centres for leprosy beggars and was looking for help in funding them. These were in virgin bush country and several hundred beggars had been collected from the streets and resettled there. The question was whether The Leprosy Mission would organise and finance another.

Much of Ethiopia is a high, dry plateau and very beautiful, although beauty is best appreciated on a full stomach, something most Ethiopians didn't have. Much of the land is subject to famine, and most of the people live in grinding poverty. It also has one of the oldest Christian traditions in the world. A long-held belief suggests that the Queen of Sheba came from Ethiopia and that she visited King Solomon in Israel. Whatever the truth of that, the Christian faith became the state religion in 330 A.D. But for many centuries it was isolated, surrounded by Muslim states and became increasingly introspective and defensive.

Around Addis the air was fresh and clear, the sunlight soft and benevolent. The landscape colours glowed with warmth. Rolling hills were yellow with crops and the old gold of drying grass. There were shaggy groves of purple-blue eucalyptus trees scenting the air, fast-growing and good for fuel. We drove out of the city, Ernest Price, plus a driver and me, heading north in a well-loaded vehicle. Ernest was Welsh, a doctor, a skilled musician and employed by the Ethiopian Health Department as a leprosy specialist.

At first the road slid smoothly over the contours and on to the wide, open plain. The land was dotted with small *tukuls*, round wattle-and-thatch houses. People walked the road, men in white cotton shirts and jodhpur trousers, women in white, calf-length pleated skirts, their black hair usually bound in brilliant coloured scarves. They wore chunky necklaces, often with a large silver cross showing their allegiance to the church.

A few local dignitaries passed by proudly on horseback, brandishing fly swats of horsehair. Their mounts were small and not always well fed but splendidly caparisoned in a bright red webbing of cloth and leather over their hindquarters, and a hand-carved wooden saddle with high pommels front and back. Children wore very little except for a string with an amulet around the neck, but were covered in flies. These congregated around the eyes and noses of babies and toddlers who seemed to accept them as a fact of life.

Further on the trees grew sparser, the country wilder and less cultivated. Birds abounded. Russet-coloured hawks hovered high, black-headed ibis pecked their way through the odd patch of marshy ground, and splendid starlings preened feathers that reflected light like shot silk. Four hours' drive from Addis the road drops with a gasp into the gorge of the Blue Nile. Millennia of erosion and natural energy have cut the gorge deeper and deeper as the river swirls down from its origin in Lake Tana. Packs of baboons crashed heavily through the undergrowth.

The driver was part-way through a full day of fasting – a big thing in the Orthodox Church. His driving was becoming increasingly erratic. He seemed to change gear for the simple pleasure of it, not because the road demanded it. He would cruise along a flat piece of road at 40 miles an hour, then suddenly change into third with a wild revving of engine, throwing us forward. Then he'd continue at 20 until bored and change into top gear just as we were approaching a steep descent.

The road dropped 4,000 feet in a few miles of hairpin bends. It was dramatic enough without the driver adding to it. Dr. Price seemed unconcerned but I was in the front passenger seat with no seat belt and I'd bought a return air ticket! I didn't want to waste it. I asked them if we could stop the car. As diplomatically as possible, I said that I loved driving mountain roads and please could I give the driver a rest? Dr. Price just smiled, so I asked the driver to change places and I took over. It was little different from driving in the Himalayas, which I'd been used to.

We laboured up the other side of the gorge and after a few more miles reached Debra Marcos. It was a ramshackle place which could have been used as a frontier town in a Western cowboy film. It was being developed, some of the work being done by prisoners from the local jail, walking and working in leg irons. The town square was busy, people and donkeys and a great confusion of noise. Herds of goats and sheep. Their herd boys wore roughly made capes of sheepskin, wool side out, to supplement their thin cotton shirts against the cold nights. The further we went from Addis Ababa the more animal skin took the place of cotton. Life was basic. And smelly.

We spent the night at a small general hospital. It was well run by a Bulgarian doctor working under an agreement between the then Communist Government of Bulgaria and the Ethiopian authorities. He spoke good English and welcomed us. The hospitality was well timed. For the last part of the drive I'd been feeling increasingly unwell. It came to a violent climax during the night. The situation had its funny side though. After a bout of nausea my camp bed collapsed as I was trying to wriggle back into my sleeping bag. Earlier in the day we'd stopped at a small local settlement. We were dehydrated and needed some liquid. The water was unsafe and Dr. Price had advised the locally-brewed beer. He assured me no germs could live in it. He was wrong and told me later I was the first mission worker he'd ever diagnosed with acute alcoholic gastritis.

In the morning we visited the Orthodox Church to pay our respects to the *Abuna*, the highly influential provincial archbishop. He had fine-drawn features, aquiline and ascetic from much fasting. Grey hair under a black satin pillbox hat. A black outer robe covered his dark brown cassock, and a large intricately fashioned silver cross hung on a cord from his neck. The church stood in its own grounds, a circular building with an overhanging roof hung with bells. Inside, the space was divided by another wall, hexagonal in design and pierced with arches. The atmosphere was heavy with incense and dust, shadows collecting in the corners, the lighting low and mysterious. A screen and iron gate shielded the holy of holies from sight.

Every inch of wall space was covered with religious paintings, stylised pictures to teach the illiterate the stories of faith. Beginning with Adam and Eve they went through the Bible and on to incidents from the lives of saints. These included St. George, the patron saint of Ethiopia as well as England. The paintings had a Byzantine flavour, overlaid by their own vernacular character, but were full of life. There was another life too, common in rural Ethiopia.

Dr. Price caught a couple of fleas on his trouser bottoms. This time they ignored me. Later I wasn't so lucky.

We drove another 50 miles to Fenote Selam. We visited a 40-bed government leprosy hospital, well built and equipped through relief money from Sweden. The Ethiopian staff had been there for two years without a single patient. The government hadn't budgeted for the cost of medicines or food. Five miles away was the site suggested for the proposed leprosy rehabilitation settlement. The only thing in its favour was the river, a turgid stream of brown water, heavy with silt. The rest was inhospitable bush, scrubby thorn trees and stony ground. I was non-committal. To expect any group of people to become self-sufficient in three years on land like this was impractical. To think of former leprosy patients with their handicaps clearing the bush, ripping out rocks, ploughing and planting, was worse.

Later in the week I was driven south by another expatriate in the leprosy service to Tibela, a functioning agricultural leprosy settlement. Unfortunately he'd never been there and didn't know the way. Two hours' drive took us to an American Mennonite Hospital. They couldn't spare anyone to guide us but the doctor drew a vague spider's web of directions on a scrap of paper. "You'll find it," he said. He must have been a very busy doctor. We drove off in the joy of ignorance, with me clutching the 'map'.

Tibela lay on the other side of 20 miles of arid waste. The stony ground was flat and featureless, covered in a tangle of desiccated thorn bush, bisected occasionally by narrow animal tracks. Every few miles the dust showed a few feet of tyre track to prove that this was a road, but mostly there was nothing. Just the sun and the dust that trailed behind us in a choking golden plume. Once or twice we met small groups of Muslim Galla tribesmen, thin and dark, hard and suspicious, carrying long spears and swords. We tried to ask our way but were met by uncomprehending silence. They hadn't heard about entertaining angels unaware.

The sun helped us keep a sense of direction and we knew that we had to cross a river somewhere ahead. We found it after a backtrack of several miles. It was the Awash and it actually had a bridge. The Tibela site was nearby. Like the other settlements it was expected to become self-sufficient after a few years of work. It was an impossible aim involving heavy and damaging labour by former leprosy patients with anaesthetic and vulnerable hands and feet. They were a sad group. They were cared for by a community of nuns who were very loving but had little experience or knowledge of the care and prevention of leprosy disability. Few of the workers had all their fingers or toes. They were mostly malnourished, heavily bandaged and incapable of the heavy work needed to establish the settlement. Self-sufficiency was out of the question.

It was a deeply depressing experience which the momentary excitement of spotting a band of black and white colobus monkeys did nothing to relieve. I began to have doubts about this type of project; good leprosy work demanded more than putting patients into isolated communities with little regard either for their dignity or their future well-being.

Next day we returned to Addis by another route. This time we had a better map but a worse road. There was no bridge on this road, and the Land Rover had to be eased down into the riverbed over rough volcanic rocks. It was like driving down the steps of St. Paul's Cathedral in London, although the rocks were far more irregular.

Back in Addis I found a small but influential group of people had congregated. They included Drs. Paul Brand and Ernest Price, and others from several voluntary agencies. They wanted to improve the standards of leprosy care not only in Ethiopia but elsewhere. They were interested in creating a new training centre which would serve all Africa, or at least all Anglophone countries on the continent. A lot of preparatory investigation had been done and Ethiopia was chosen as a country politically stable as far as could be seen. Looking back a better choice might have been made, but it had a number of quiet years to develop before the violent Marxist revolution which came later. The centre that was created worked right through those tense days.

I was invited to join the group. They proposed a training centre to be based on the Princess Zenebework Leprosy Hospital in Addis itself. This was a large, comparatively well-staffed government centre but it was short of money and ripe for improvement. The aim was to take it over and develop it as a teaching and research centre together with control programmes and a strong emphasis on rehabilitation. It would be known as ALERT, the All Africa Leprosy and Rehabilitation Training Centre.

The impressions I'd been forming crystallised. The idea was exciting and had a strategic potential far beyond any agricultural settlements. I felt the Mission should be part of it. I dropped any thought of agricultural projects and signed as one of the four founding members of ALERT. It was way beyond my brief to tie the Mission into this, but if I'd sent telegrams back to London they might have said no. I didn't want to risk that. On my return to London I reported back. Eyebrows were raised, objections made. I hadn't the authority to commit the Mission to a scheme this big and the Mission didn't usually involve itself in schemes with secular rather than specifically Christian partners anyway. I held my ground and the commitment to ALERT was honoured. The agricultural schemes we left alone.

As a member of ALERT's Board of Governors for a number of years there were some difficult and frustrating times working through the insecurity and violence of the Ethiopian Marxist revolution in the mid 1970s. But ALERT grew into a formidable and widely-respected training centre with a worldwide influence. Its training has transformed the picture of leprosy in many parts of Africa and beyond. The Leprosy Mission has contributed to it greatly over the years. Not in great financial terms, but in skilled and experienced workers who've contributed a lot to ALERT's development.

On one visit I met the Emperor, Haile Selassie, a very powerful personality in a fairly small body. Actually, I first saw him in Nottingham when I was ten years old, just before World War II began. The authorities had staged a spectacular outdoor pageant in the grounds of an Elizabethan manor house. It was a selective and highly patriotic enactment of British history from Roman times on. As children we cheered Boudicca in her chariot but the official highlight was the visit of Haile Selassie. He was then living in exile in England, the victim of Mussolini's conquest of his country. I had no idea then what the future held as I stood cheering.

Neither had he. He returned to Ethiopia after the war's end and resumed his reign, but just a few years after ALERT began he was deposed, held in prison and allegedly murdered by suffocation. Living and working in Addis during this revolution was difficult. I only experienced it as an occasional visitor and admired and respected those who worked faithfully and loyally through the violence of those years.

Even a visit could have moments of tension. One evening I'd been invited by Jean Watson, the TLM physiotherapist, to a Bible study group which met in the city. Driving back in the dark we were stopped by a group of local vigilantes. They weren't in any uniform but they were armed, one of many such cells set up by the revolutionary government to enforce its will. They were often trigger-happy, particularly at night. Jean pulled over. "Just show them your passport," she said. "We'll be all right." My passport was safely locked in a suitcase in my bedroom. No one had told me it was a good idea to carry it. Jean showed hers. I looked down at the open glove compartment in the dashboard of the car. There was an official looking document there, the car's logbook. I took a chance, picked it up and showed it through the window. Literacy isn't widespread in Ethiopia. The man looked at it briefly and waved us on.

On several visits to Ethiopia I flew with Missionary Aviation Fellowship. On one occasion my baggage was limited to ten pounds, as many of the airstrips were at altitudes of 9,000 feet above sea level and the small single-engined Cessnas could carry only limited loads at those heights. As if that wasn't enough, an emergency call for help was radioed through while we were in the air. We diverted, and I was dumped on an isolated plateau miles from anywhere while the pilot flew off to pick up a doctor and ferry him to deal with a cholera outbreak. There were no houses, no people, no movement of any kind. My imagination worked overtime, wondering "What if..." I sat and listened intently for an hour for the welcome sound of the plane returning.

My frequent travels in Africa over the next few years emphasised the strategic timing of ALERT. When I visited leprosy centres I went with two purposes in mind. The first was to find out what was going on and how TLM's money was being spent. It was fair to say that until that time, our emphasis had been on Southern Asia, particularly India and Nepal, and on Hong Kong and Korea in East Asia.

In most African countries our role was almost totally restricted to making grants of money to enable others to do the leprosy work. Many of the centres we were helping had been left to get on with it, with few visits from TLM representatives for several years or longer. I wanted to put that right. As I travelled my reactions were mixed. Wherever I went I found workers from a wide variety of missions, dedicated to the care of leprosy patients but many of whom had little knowledge of modern developments in treatment. I had come from India, where things were far from perfect but where rapid progress was being made. African countries, with a few honourable exceptions, were way behind. It called for some diplomacy. Here were folk working hard in the best way they knew. It wasn't easy as a newcomer whose experience had been in Asia to breeze into African situations and suggest that there were better ways of doing things. But that's why ALERT had been founded.

This gave a second reason for my visits – to encourage workers, often very isolated, to raise their standards of care. There was a lot of ground to be made up, particularly in the prevention of deformity and foot care. We had great help from Dr. Stanley Browne. He had a lifetime's experience in Africa and was, at this time, Director of the Leprosy Study Centre in London. Stanley was an impressive personality. A powerful mix of firm Christian commitment and strong egotism which didn't make him the easiest person to work with. But he had a gigantic appetite for work, was well known on the international leprosy scene, and was an inspiring teacher. As our Medical Consultant he travelled tirelessly and his teaching greatly strengthened the Mission's medical work and image.

I visited Lambarene in Gabon, West Africa, the almost legendary hospital set up by Albert Schweitzer on the edge of the Ogooue River. The humidity was intense. We were almost at sea level and only fifty miles from the equator. Wide and brown, the river held in its grasp blue sky and cumulus clouds in reflection. Palm trees cordoned the banks like policemen holding the crowding rainforest at bay. The hospital itself was rambling, dark and smoky and overrun by goats. Its ethos was always controversial. Schweitzer's vision was to keep conditions as near to African village levels as possible so that sick people would feel at home. It was thought that an alien and antiseptic environment could threaten them, but the management was heavily paternalistic and the newly independent government were expecting change.

The leprosy village which was part of the hospital was a sad place that both moved and frustrated me. Most patients were old and burnt out with tragic deformities. The staff were kind but no one showed any enthusiasm for change, although one doctor was using DDS. But it was all very small-scale. What was worse from my viewpoint was that a senior executive from the European Friends of Lambarene Committee was visiting at the same time and advising them to reduce the work. The first thing he suggested reducing was, of course, the care of leprosy sufferers.

Gifts from patients in Zaire – a pineapple and a live chicken, 1986

To compensate I had the joy of spending several hours with a baby gorilla. At least I was told she was a baby. She was about 30 inches tall, weighed about 40 pounds and was strong. Her mother had been shot illegally by a hunter from whom the baby had been rescued. She was a gorgeous creature – the gorilla not the hunter – with intelligent soft brown eyes set deep in a black leathery face. She had thick coarse hair and delicate hands with small finger nails.

It can be very difficult getting away from an affectionate gorilla. The thing she wanted most was close living contact. We sat at the foot of a palm tree in a warm embrace. The embrace began as a voluntary affair between two consenting parties but it was a relationship I found difficult to terminate. The difficulty was physical. How do you detach a reluctant gorilla which can hold on with all or any one of its four limbs when I could only react with two? Eventually she turned a somersault, using my chest as a jumping off ground, stood in front of me and thumped her chest as gorillas do – on television anyway. I was glad I never met her mother.

Another journey took me through the Congo as it then was, soon to be renamed Zaire and

The village pond
West Bengal, India
Watercolour
1964

now back to Congo again. It was a country with problems on a massive scale. Travel and communication were difficult. There was some excellent medical work being done at the Institut Médical Evangélique in Kimpese near the capital Kinshasa. This was a large general hospital run by a group of Christian missions. The leprosarium at nearby Kivuvu was an integral part of its work.

Kivuvu was run by Dr. Wayne Meyers together with an English Baptist nursing sister, Edna Staple. Meyers was a resourceful, highly skilled and imaginative American missionary doctor, softly spoken but determined. He had a

quirky sense of humour. He arranged a major journey around the country for the two of us to get to know what was happening and how better The Leprosy Mission could help. We already gave financial help to a number of leprosy centres in Congo but we had little idea of what they did. They sent annual reports but having written many myself I know that what's not said is as important as what is. We travelled widely, by commercial airline and in single-engined planes landing on small airstrips hacked out of the rainforest. Land Rovers took us on muddy forest tracks and we had narrow scrapes with rotten log bridges and in dugout canoes.

On one journey we had to cross the River Congo. There had been a great storm in the afternoon and we delayed the crossing hoping the rain would blow over. It did but not until late in the day. We bargained for spaces in a *pirogue*, a 25-foot long dugout canoe with an outboard motor. It was already packed with ten people and two crew but they made room for us and our bags and we pushed off from shore. The river was wide, five miles across, the sky still stormy, the water the colour of pewter. We had a mere six inches of freeboard when we were stationary. When the motor began it pushed the prow of the canoe higher but the main hull sank into the water and the freeboard almost disappeared. The bow wave splashed in as the rain began again.

Out in midstream with rain pouring down we could see neither bank. I unhitched my cameras from around my neck thinking they'd weigh me down if I had to swim for it. I eyed the great clumps of water hyacinth floating by and wondered if they'd support my weight. The sky darkened even more as dusk approached and with no visibility we seemed in limbo. Then suddenly through the murk we saw a few lights, more precious than diamonds. The boatman cut the engine and we nosed gently into the shore. I'm not sure about the dividing line between trust and recklessness but it's sometimes pretty thin. We walked up the bank in the dark through rushes and long wet grass. Fireflies danced a wild green fluorescent welcome and behind them a Land Rover waited for us.

It was shortly after the Simba uprising when the Belgian colonial administration had pulled out with limited notice and the country was in chaos. Large parts had been overrun by rebels before order of a sort was restored. Hospitals, clinics and schools had been looted and destroyed and many people killed. Most of the medical infrastructure had disappeared, although there were many Zairois medical assistants faithfully working at their posts with almost no supplies and no payment but doing all they could to help their own people.

Excellent work had been done in the past by pioneers like Dr. Stanley Browne in the area around Kisangani in the north-east but most of that too had been destroyed. Even the medical records had gone. Sometimes the conditions in which patients were living were heartbreaking. Some had simply disappeared into the forest. Others had been gathered together into self-regulatory villages, the better to be treated by the few medical staff nearby but the standards were often appalling, almost medieval. Something had to be done. Even though the primary responsibility wasn't ours I felt deeply ashamed that we were doing so little to improve things.

In spite of this the hospitality offered by patients was moving. At one leprosy village we'd met sufferers at every stage of disability, living hand-to-mouth with little food. As we left an old man approached me. He spoke halting French. He thanked me for coming and for taking an interest in them all. "We would like you to have this," he said, holding something hidden between his hands. I put out my hands, cupped to receive. He gave me a single small egg laid by one of the scrawny chickens scratching round their huts. It was all they could give and they gave it with dignity. My first reaction was to say, "No thank you. You keep it. You need it more than I do." But I realised how important it was that they should feel able to give, to offer hospitality. I had so much but was shown the art of giving by people who had nothing. The egg was eaten but its memory stays with me.

In another centre we were entertained a little more lavishly to a palm oil stew of porcupine, freshly hunted in the forest, and red rice. That morning's offering at church included a smoked haunch of antelope. People had to supplement their food in any way they could. They worked vegetable gardens around their shacks even though the clearing and digging often injured their already damaged hands and feet. The fitter ones went into the forest hunting, not for pleasure but for a little meat to add variety to their diet.

There were moments during these visits when the best that we could offer seemed tragically inadequate but it was better to do something rather than nothing. There were a few centres that offered the possibility of improvement given training, encouragement and money.

But the situation needed new energy on the spot. Back in London I recommended that we look for a doctor to head up a renewed attempt to help in Zaire as it had just been renamed and to bring some order out of the chaos. It would be a tough job. I remembered Dr. John and Elsie Harris, deeply committed missionaries who had worked in Zaire but had had to leave during the violence. Subsequently they had joined TLM and had done first-class work, firstly in South India and at this time in Nepal. John excelled in pioneering situations rather than routine ones and I wondered how he'd feel about a return to Africa.

He was non-committal. I suggested he do a reconnaissance at TLM's expense. He went, came back, talked and prayed with his family and volunteered to go. We stationed him in the north-east at Nyankunde, another joint venture mission hospital. Before long we were negotiating with Missionary Aviation Fellowship to organise a regular series of leprosy clinics by air to overcome the constant difficulties and dangers of road travel. It worked and before long John was organising training courses for local paramedical workers and encouraging them in their work.

There was encouragement in Uganda. Visiting Kuluva in the north-west a short time before Idi Amin came to power, I found the Williams brothers, both doctors, doing excellent work and up to date in their knowledge of leprosy. Again I flew with MAF. The airstrip was surrounded by hills and the approach was made difficult by a bank of tall trees at one end. We circled twice, high and low, and came in down hill, barely skimming the trees. There was a strong cross wind. The plane was difficult to control. We hit hard, bounced and the wind got under one wing. It lifted. The other wing was inches from the ground and we were close to tragedy. With a great effort the pilot regained control and we slewed to a stop. "Will you say a prayer?" he asked. I already had.

Ted, the elder of the two doctor brothers, was also an honorary government game warden and took me out one day to look for white rhino. There were few left in the area and he was protecting them with enthusiasm. The *white* refers not to its colour, because it's grey like other rhino, but comes from the Afrikaans *weit*, meaning wide. It describes its big square jaw.

We travelled some distance by four-wheel drive then walked. The African tracker spotted something. We followed. Ahead was a large male rhino over five feet high at the shoulder and with a massive horn. We circled quietly to get downwind of him and slowly got nearer. Ted had a .300 rifle for protection in dire emergency but was very reluctant to use it. His advice, in case we were charged, was to stand our ground until the last minute, then run at right angles to the rhino's direction. "They're so heavy," he said, "once they're up to full speed they can't swerve."

I wasn't keen to test the theory but I wanted some photographs. I stood up in the knee-high grass but the rhino heard the camera shutter clicking. He turned, pawed the ground, tossed his head and began to move. "Shout," said Ted and we all did, and clapped our hands. Whether it scared him or he just accepted it as applause I never knew, but he turned and lumbered off. On the walk back we were soaked by a sudden tropical rainstorm but we saw warthog, a timid duiker and several other antelope.

CHAPTER TWELVE
Film Making

When we were home on leave from India in 1962 Newberry Fox - our children called him Newberry Fruit – was the Mission's Promotional Secretary. He was responsible for publicity and fund-raising. He suggested that we make a film of the work in Purulia for home use. I'd done a lot of still photography and was very enthusiastic, although I quickly learned the great difference between still and movie photography. Walter Fancutt, the Mission's Editorial Secretary, and I wrote a script which I took back to India. It was to be based on the life of Gunanidhi, one of our long-term patients. He'd had leprosy since childhood and through his story we intended to show the positive changes in leprosy care that had taken place since then.

We found a professional film producer in Bombay. He was an Italian named Carlo Marconi and he'd done some work for Paul Brand. Carlo was a stereotypical Italian, although I suspect he played up the image for his own amusement. He was temperamental and volatile but a perfectionist in his film work. He threw out our script and together we wrote a new one. The story was to be the same but the approach quite different. As a lapsed Roman Catholic Carlo had strange ideas about the church and mission. We had several arguments in which I had to tell him that bishops and clergy in long flowing robes weren't really appropriate to this particular film and we didn't have many anyway. I think he'd seen too many Hollywood epics.

Some of our patients volunteered as actors to show Guna's life. Carlo's attitude changed. With inexperienced actors he was gentle and encouraging, reserving the histrionics for me. We had our moments though. One day we were trying to shoot a simple scene of Guna as a boy of ten herding his family's cattle and goats. He was to sit under a tree playing a flute, the animals grazing behind him.

There's no such thing as a simple scene in movie making. We chose the tree. The boy sat with his flute and the cattle were released behind him. They wandered as the camera rolled. They were driven back. They didn't like it and refused to stay. More film wasted. We put down cut grass to tempt them. It worked, the camera rolled again but at the last minute of the shot a stray patient wandered through the scene. Cut! Several deep breaths later we tried again. It went perfectly and without a hitch until the last moment when the film stock in the camera ran out. Carlo stood up, his face deep red behind his silver beard. Raising shaking hands to heaven he looked up, ready to explode. "Mama mia!" he shouted. The scene had taken two hours to set up and photograph and would occupy about ten seconds in the finished film. I said it was time for coffee.

Carlo's life had been colourful. He'd left Italy for India in the late 1930s because he didn't like Fascism, but when Italy entered World War Two he was arrested by the British as an enemy alien. He was interned with other Italians in a camp at Dehra Dun. He had many stories. The food the British army gave them wasn't very good. Among the internees was a chef from the Lloyd Triestino shipping line. They persuaded the authorities to give them dry rations and they organised their own kitchen. They adapted an old clothes mangle to make fresh pasta. They also managed to pass food over to the German side of the camp, and helped Heinrich Harrer escape to Tibet where he became tutor to the young Dalai Lama (his story is told in Harrer's autobiography, *Seven Years in Tibet*).

Carlo said he didn't like the discipline the British imposed. "If Mussolini couldn't make me march, no one could." He told too of their way with postage stamps when they were allowed to write home from India through the Red Cross. "We didn't lick the stamps," he told me, "we spat on them." Seeing my blank look he explained. "They had your king's head on them."

Relaxing from the film making one evening I asked him if he would teach me to make pasta and Bolognese sauce from scratch. He was enthusiastic. Within minutes the kitchen was in chaos with flour, eggs and water all over the place. Our cook was wide-eyed and disbelieving. The pasta was rolled out, and rolled again. "Thinner, thinner," shouted Carlo. He cut it into strings and festooned the kitchen with it, a culinary Christmas, pasta hanging everywhere to dry. We had loads of tomatoes, locally grown. In the excitement his English could be colourful. He watched the sauce cooking in its pan. "Hmm," he said, stroking his beard, "she is boiling, how you say, a little too emotionally."

Film-making in Purulia – Carlo Marconi
prepares his camera

The filming ended, I spent time with him in Bombay for the editing. It was his turn to try my patience as we wrestled with both pictures and script. Every small detail had to be right for Carlo but it was worth it. It was the first professional film the Mission had made and it won first prize out of 38 entries for a film on rehabilitation at an International Society for Rehabilitation of the Disabled exhibition in Wiesbaden in Germany. The result of my time in **Bom**bay wasn't so good. Back in Purulia I came down with typhoid for the second time.

The film was successful in education and fund-raising and we looked around later for a follow-up. I suggested Korea. TLM's work there had been disrupted by the Korean War in the early 1950s but in the uneasy peace that followed a new team of TLM workers had begun to revive it. Together with a growing group of outstanding Koreans they had developed a new hospital in Taegu, one of the country's major cities. They were also doing significant work in health education and rehabilitation.

Korea, 'Land of Morning Calm', is a beautiful and mountainous country full of wonderful people. The Christian Church was expanding rapidly among a nominally Buddhist population. On visiting South Korea, I had been moved by the sight of a bridge that spanned the 38th Parallel at Panmunjom, the cease-fire line and border between North and South Korea. Folk called it 'The Bridge of No Return' because any one who managed to cross in either direction stood little chance of getting back. It seemed a metaphor for what leprosy had been in many tragic lives and we based the story on it, calling the film *Bridge of Return*. It won a gold medal for Hugh Baddeley, the producer, from the Royal Photographic Society.

Sometime before the Korean film, I had visited Kumi, a leprosy centre the Mission supported in north-east Uganda. I met an outstanding patient there. His name was Livingstone Chekweko. He was very tall and thin, his hands and feet badly damaged by leprosy. He had a severe facial paralysis and when I first saw him he was in a hospital bed. But he was painting. He held a brush between the stumps of thumb and fingers, a large sheet of paper in front of him. I was intrigued. His paintings were naive, untutored, but strong and direct. He painted scenes of local village life and dramatic pictures of wild animals in the bush.

He'd lived as a child in a village on the slopes of Mount Elgon. His mother had died while he was a baby and he was brought up by his father and elder sister. He went to the local school. One day, looking at a tattered copy of a printed magazine he was fascinated by the photographs. Real life could be depicted in two dimensions on paper. It was a turning point in his life. He began to draw secretly on any bit of paper he could find.

Then leprosy struck. Knowing how people reacted to it he retreated to the edge of the village. He built his own hut, a simple framework of lopped branches tied together with creepers and string, and roofed with grass. There was no more school. His family sent him food, but he was lonely. From time to time he was gripped by episodes of painful fever but when he felt well he went on drawing. He experimented with colours made from berries and leaves. He chewed twigs to make brushes.

His health deteriorated. The local healer couldn't help and one day Livingstone took a great chance. He hitched a lift in a truck and came to Kumi. He was taken in and was fortunate in meeting Jane Neville, the occupational therapist. She encouraged his painting and gave him better materials. Jane was to make a very significant contribution to leprosy work in later years. After some years in Kumi she became a key worker in ALERT in Addis Ababa, and later joined TLM's

International Office staff in London as Education and Training Director. She travelled widely, training and inspiring workers in modern teaching methods.

Livingstone developed a strong Christian faith. His health improved and his courage inspired other patients. A few years later his artistic ability was recognised more widely and he exhibited in Kampala and appeared on Ugandan television.

Taking his story as a basis, I wrote a script. The workers at Kumi were cooperative so I hired a two-man film crew – a director/cameraman and a sound man – and we flew out. The film began well but there was a sudden crisis to face. John, the cameraman, developed a tummy upset and had to use the lavatory several times in the night. The lavatory was one of the prettiest I've seen. It was outside at the bottom of the garden, had a petrol blue door and an arching bougainvillaea creeper showering magenta petals all over it. The trouble was the cockroaches.

It was a simple bore hole latrine. As John entered shining his torch in the dark the light attracted the cockroaches. John didn't want to share his misery with them. Next morning he complained to me over breakfast. I consulted but was met with amused shrugs. "This is Africa," we were reminded. The next night the same thing happened. John was an artistic and sensitive man and at breakfast it was apparent that he wasn't used to this and was ready to pack up and go home. He wasn't used to African wildlife, even the small stuff.

I spoke to one of the staff and asked firmly that something should be done. He agreed and we met later at the latrine. He carried half a gallon of kerosene, a newspaper and matches. He poured the kerosene through the small circular hole below the lavatory seat. Then he made a large twist of newspaper, lit it and pushed the flaming paper down the hole. There was a pause when I thought it wasn't going to work. Then with a rumble that turned into a great explosion, the blast sent scorching hot air up through the loo just as my friend was looking down. We had no more trouble with cockroaches and I believe my colleague's eyebrows grew back eventually.

We called the film *How Great A Flame*. This had nothing to do with the sudden death of the cockroaches but was a quote from a Wesley hymn on how great things can come from small beginnings.

Worshippers at north Indian temple
Watercolour
2000

CHAPTER THIRTEEN
Taking Over

Newberry Fox retired as the Mission's International General Secretary in 1974. After a number of candidates had been looked at, I was asked to succeed him. It challenged me but I felt I could do it. I've never actively sought promotion but I've always said yes when asked to take on extra responsibility. Sometimes I've taken it without waiting to be asked if I've seen a gap that needed filling. I felt I could do it as well as anyone else and I knew leprosy from working at the sharp end - in the field. The challenge was in seeing the bigger picture and providing the stimulus and opportunity for others to develop the work. In creating the space that would give them the freedom they needed.

But there were significant problems to be faced. I'd learnt a lot working with Newberry, particularly in the diplomatic handling of people. Newberry had great qualities. He was a warm-hearted enthusiast. Not always the coolest in thought, he threw himself wholeheartedly into any project that caught his attention. His motives were always the best but he had a great talent for stepping on toes, and frequently couldn't understand why folk were upset with him. A lot of my work as his deputy had been liaising with Audrey Pyle, his very capable personal assistant, and explaining him to those he'd hurt.

He'd done a good job extending the Mission's appeal to church groups in Western Europe, notably in France, Germany and the Netherlands. This was later consolidated and expanded into other countries by a very talented Italian, Silvano Perotti, who also played a key role in establishing the Mission in parts of Eastern Europe. Not an easy thing to do. Newberry was an ideas man. He had ten ideas a day and, as was said of Winston Churchill, at least one of them was good. The problem was spotting the good one and helping him to forget the rest. Like many ideas-people he had a breadth of vision but little patience or ability to work out the detail. That was left to me.

One immediate challenge had raised its head several months before while Newberry was still in charge. Barbara and I were invited to New Zealand to meet members of the Mission's New Zealand Council and to speak to many of its supporters. It was a hectic visit. In less than four weeks we spoke at 47 meetings and slept in 20 different beds. There were church congregations, large and small weekday meetings, radio and television interviews. We managed to fit in a number of other events such as a white water journey on the Shotover River in a jet boat and some more relaxing moments, visiting Maori cultural centres, and meeting Douglas Badcock, one of New Zealand's leading landscape painters. But underneath it all there was great tension.

The Mission was and is international. It welcomes support of all kinds – people, prayer and money – from any part of the world. But at this time its governing body was almost entirely English, male and middle class. It was not only English but almost completely Home Counties English, made up of folk who could meet regularly in London. It was a practical arrangement and the members were fine people but their vision didn't yet recognise the feelings of supporters in other countries. There were regular consultations across borders but all significant decisions, and many smaller ones too, were made in London.

There were increasing protests about this, particularly from Australia and New Zealand. They had a growing interest in meeting the needs of leprosy sufferers in Papua New Guinea and Indonesia but London didn't always respond with the speed and positive action the area needed. These protests came to a head during our New Zealand visit. The issue had arisen once before and Newberry had dealt with it legalistically, relying on the Mission's Constitution to control and hold people together.

It hadn't worked. The genuine goodwill and fellowship within the Mission was being eroded by the frustration of distance and the feeling of remote supporters that their voice wasn't being heard. There were some tough discussions while we were in New Zealand and independence was talked about reluctantly but seriously. I realised that the Mission was in real danger of breaking up. We were left in no doubt about it.

On my return to London I tried to explain the depth of feeling to Newberry but it was hard going. He wasn't able to hear what was being said. He thought I was 'taking their side'. I was angry and desperate. I took a deep breath and went over his head. I asked for an interview with the chairman, Sir Harry Greenfield. It wasn't the thing to do. He didn't like it but he listened and I was able to get the Council, rather reluctantly, to set up a new international committee with a wide membership. They hedged its powers with restrictions but it was a beginning. Within a few years it grew into the International Executive Committee which is now the driving force within the Mission. There was no split. The unity of the Mission was preserved and we began to learn from each other in a new and exciting way. It released a flood of energy and creativity which gave a new impetus to the work.

From this experience I proposed an international conference for TLM representatives worldwide. It wouldn't be cheap and TLM wasn't used to spending money on what, in those days, were referred to as international junkets. I felt it was vital. We needed to take a deep and wide-ranging look together at all the Mission's policies and programmes and set management objectives we could all agree on. It took two years of careful planning but we met in Singapore in 1976.

Morgan Derham, TLM's Communications Director, played a crucial role in the planning as did other members of the International Office. Morgan was a powerful character. He had wide experience in the management of

Christian organisations. As a writer he was rapid, lucid, concise and inspiring. He walked alone, carving out his own path, but he and I worked together very well.

The *Deed and Word* document that came out of the conference set the Mission's agenda for the next decade. There were sparky debates, even on the conference theme itself, *Deed and Word*. Some wanted *Word and Deed*, arguing that evangelism was the first priority. Others believed that Deed – in our case the medical and social care we offered – had to prepare the way and validate the Word. Most of us reached a deeper understanding that deed often is word, and that what we do and how we do it speaks louder than what we say. After all, Jesus is described as the Word and he did a lot more than preach. It seems to me that there can never be one 'right' order in a varied and changing world.

Providing people with help that has no strings attached is valid in itself even when there's no opportunity to talk openly about the faith. And to withhold medical care from desperately ill people because a government puts restrictions on preaching seems to me to be wildly un-Christian. Even in areas where restrictions are severe, lives can still be changed. Experience in several countries has proved that.

There was also need to look at other areas into which TLM could expand, using resources that had built up over the years. We'd been rather cautious in our approach but several new fields were opening up, particularly in Papua New Guinea and Indonesia. This was a result of the new dynamism from TLM Australia and New Zealand, whose leaders were showing great enthusiasm now that they were being taken seriously by the Mission.

I still missed the daily contact with patients although the thrill of being able to influence the central development of the Mission made up for it.

After the Singapore Conference Barbara and I continued on our first round-the-world trip. We spent time in Hong Kong and Korea. Across the Pacific we caught our breath briefly in Hawaii. We visited Olaf Skinsnes, an erudite American doctor of Scandinavian origin. He had worked with the Mission in Hong Kong but was now working within the Medical School of the University of Hawaii. He ran the Leprosy Atelier, financed by the American Leprosy Missions.

His laboratory was unique. It combined the two major interests in his life, highly technical research into leprosy and Chinese art. I'd never seen a laboratory like it. The lab walls were painted Chinese vermilion, the doors carved and painted with beautiful abstracts inspired by what could be seen through his microscope. There were Chinese scroll paintings everywhere.

Olaf had a state of the art electron microscope and was pursuing every leprosy worker's dream, the *in vitro* cultivation of the leprosy bacillus – attempting to grow the germ in glass in the laboratory as this would open up the possible development of a vaccine, and could help in both diagnosis and treatment. No one had ever done it convincingly but Olaf was certain he'd succeeded. He showed us a dozen small conical glass flasks, each a third full of amber liquid with a light sediment in the bottom. This, he was sure, was made up of the bacilli. They certainly were bacilli of some sort but sadly his work couldn't be replicated by other workers in other laboratories.

Our visit to Hawaii was short. We'd dreamt for some time of a visit to Molokai, the island where Hawaii's leprosy sufferers had been isolated in earlier years and where Father Damien had worked. He'd caught leprosy himself and died among them. But time seemed too short until we mentioned it to Olaf.

One of his daughters was doing a research project on Molokai so we hired a light aircraft and flew over the next morning. A 20-minute flight over the water brought us to the island, about 30-miles long and with the most spectacular and forbidding cliffs I've ever seen. Most of them 2,000 feet high, they drop sheer to the pounding surf below. Above them and at a distance, mountains rise green and lush for another 3,000 feet.

The old Kalaupapa leprosy settlement is on a promontory almost totally cut off from the rest of the island. That's why it was chosen for leprosy work in the 1850s. On the landward side the mountains create their own obstacle, especially for weak and disabled patients. Along the cliffs the water crashes onto the rocks with great force. There's always a heavy swell. There are no beaches. Boats can land on only a few favourable days each year.

In Victorian times patients were collected twice a year, taken from Hawaii to Molokai by boat and if necessary forced off into deep water. If they made it to shore that was all right. If they didn't, well, they were only leprosy sufferers and didn't really matter. Disabled as they were, the first 70 patients to be sent there were left to fend for themselves. Half of them died within weeks.

Slowly the settlement built up, lawless and unsupervised. In 1873, Father Damien volunteered to live among them. That year was a very creative year for leprosy although no one realised it at the time. Three things happened widely separated by distance. As Damien, a Belgian Roman Catholic priest, was beginning his life on Molokai, an Irish Presbyterian missionary school teacher saw the suffering of leprosy patients in India. He was Wellesley Bailey and, home on leave, he challenged his friends in Ireland to support the work he'd begun. His work became The Leprosy Mission. That same year Dr. Armauer Hansen, working in a leprosarium in Bergen, Norway, announced that he'd discovered the germs that cause leprosy in skin smears taken from his patients.

Damien's story is too well documented to tell here, but he developed leprosy himself and died on Molokai after living there for 16 years. On our visit we saw his original grave, although some years ago his remains were exhumed and taken back to Belgium, a piece of religious vandalism I doubt he would have been happy with. He would have preferred to stay with the people he had loved and given his life for.

We saw the church he built and which is still in use. It houses the collection box he designed with a bell inside. The bell rang when a coin hit it so that the blind among his congregation would hear that they'd put their gifts in the right place. What they would do if the bell didn't ring I don't know and didn't ask. It also preserved the holes he cut in the floor to allow his flock to spit through.

Outside we met Alice, a 70-year-old patient of Chinese stock who arrived there when she was 19 and had never left. Fifty one years of tragic isolation. There'd been many like her. Modern patients are treated at home as outpatients but there were still a couple of hundred disabled and inactive patients living out their lives in a place that had become home. Most of the island is beautiful, much of it still wild and unspoiled, and kept by the US government as a national park.

Another journey that left its mark on me was to Bangladesh. It was a couple of years after the terrible war with Pakistan that resulted in Bangladesh's independence. Many innocent people had suffered dreadfully. At one stage ten million refugees had crossed the border into India and once the war was over many ethnic 'Biharis' – non-Bengalis who were identified with Pakistan – crowded into holding camps in Bangladesh itself. Life was tough, even tougher than it usually was.

To make things worse, many parts of the country then suffered floods which swamped their crops and ruined the harvest. Thousands of up-country people had lost everything. Their homes destroyed, they crowded into Dacca, the capital city, hoping life would be a little easier there. It wasn't.

At six o'clock one morning I visited a refugee camp run by a group from the Salvation Army. It was a large complex of unfinished warehouse buildings, bare brick walls, tin roof and mud floors. The one-acre site was wet and muddy with a large, squalid pool of green water in the centre. Everything drained into it. Conditions were primitive. People were squeezed into every corner of every building. Each family had marked out its territory, trying instinctively to preserve a little private space but as more people came in there was great overcrowding. That created tension and noisy quarrels.

It was grim. Many of the old had already died and most of the survivors were seriously malnourished. Gaunt, grey-haired men and women with flesh hardly covering their bones. The children were worse, the youngest just hanging on to life. Kwashiorkor (a tragic protein-deficiency illness brought on by malnutrition) was common. Matchstick-limbed and pot-bellied, some covered in impetigo and scabies, the children sat around, dull-eyed and listless. They were all too weak and bewildered, too beaten to do anything but sit. If anyone found energy it was to plead for a *chitti*, the magic letter of recommendation from someone in authority which would open a mythical door to work and a better life – the way things happened in Bangladesh. In one corner a team of young volunteers struggled desperately to control, discipline and feed two long lines of people. Tempers were getting raw in the noise and humidity.

There was a 'hospital' block as primitive as the rest. There was widespread dysentery and the beginnings of cholera. Measles had already begun. "That'll kill many of the children," I said, half questioning, half stating a fact and hoping to be contradicted. "Maybe that'll be better for them," said my guide with a sigh. "They don't have much to look forward to if they survive."

Not all the people would survive. As I watched two stretchers were laid out in the mud. Two men had died during the night. A grey-bearded man, sightless eyes half open, his neighbour younger. A small crowd of children gathered to stare. Death was a familiar process, there was no fear and no great curiosity. It was just a slight change in the day's routine. Another man washed the corpses, sloshing water from a battered aluminium pot, moving the bodies casually, without emotion.

Beyond the hunger, disease and the fact of death itself, the ultimate tragedy was the lack of dignity. There was no privacy either in life or death, no room for personality. Each body just another small jigsaw piece added to the total picture of suffering. It seemed to me then and still does that the restoration of human dignity was one of the most valuable things we could struggle towards in

Christian mission. It's one of the first things destroyed by calamity, natural or human-made, and its destruction upsets and angers me.

Dignity is vulnerable and is so often identified by its absence. It can be destroyed physically by pain and suffering, mentally by the grinding despair and helplessness of poverty, and spiritually by the attacks made on faith. "Does God care?" – the classic question. I believe he does, but a God who has made himself vulnerable in human form can only show his care through us. The trouble is that the Good Samaritan of the parable isn't always there. Often people simply suffer alone and without help. The Samaritan is busy elsewhere or he, too, may have been attacked on the road. Mission surely must aim to restore human dignity; to take people through their dependency on charitable help to self-sufficiency and a realisation of their own worth.

I was told that throughout the city and its camps the real figure for hunger-deaths was between 120 and 130 each night. Yet in the city life went on. There were long queues for the cinemas, and the traffic snarled up as it always did. Shops were open and doing brisk business. Food was available if you had the money. The few hotels were busy, mostly with journalists and people from the aid agencies.

It all added a sharp relevance to consultations later in the day. These were with representatives of several organisations who had begun to set up a joint project, largely under the initiative of TEAR Fund (The Evangelical Alliance Relief Fund). The project was called HEED – Health, Education and Economic Development – and was to create a number of medical and self-help employment schemes. As a result of the discussions I committed The Leprosy Mission to take responsibility for the leprosy component in the projects, a work that grew over the years into a substantial involvement in leprosy treatment, control and rehabilitation throughout a large section of the country.

TLM's work began to gather speed in other areas. In India it expanded with growing emphasis on control and rehabilitation.

More responsibilities were taken on at the government's request in Papua New Guinea and Indonesia. TLM began a significant project in the Biak Regency of Irian Jaya, which shares a common border with Papua New Guinea. It includes many islands, large and small. Roads are few and the sea is the highway. I visited the Padaidos, a group of islands two and a half hours sailing from Biak. We used the local government ambulance boat, a 30-foot narrow-hulled outrigger canoe, dug out from an enormous forest tree. It had a corrugated iron shed amidships and two engines.

Sketching in Irian Jaya

With 16 people on board we set off early in the morning. The day was bright, the sea calm. An hour out from shore the main engine died. The second, a large outboard motor was lowered and started. It ran for ten minutes and expired. Regular mechanical maintenance didn't seem to be part of the work programme. The mechanic began taking the outboard apart. For the next 90 minutes we drifted in an increasingly heavy swell, lifting and wallowing while repairs were made. A short but sharp rainstorm added to the problems and the growing realisation that we were drifting towards a coral reef over which waves were breaking. Eventually the outboard was brought back to life and we turned and ran for shore. We made a second and successful journey a couple of days later.

We waded ashore through crystal clear water teeming with enormous red and orange starfish, crimson sea urchins and brilliant turquoise fish. We set up a clinic on the edge of the village, a group of about 50 houses on stilts over the water. Several areas were demarcated. Blood smears were taken at the malaria table, stained and examined immediately by microscope. A baby clinic was set up, another for general medical problems, and a leprosy treatment clinic. While these were working, all the school-age children were examined both for leprosy and other skin conditions. When I returned to London I recommended that TLM build its own boat to avoid depending on the unreliable government boat, and that two-way radios be installed.

There was growing pressure to do more in Africa. I was doubtful and rather hesitant. There were many people needing help, but it was difficult to see how and where conditions would allow the regularity of treatment needed for it to be effective. Alan Waudby, TLM's conscientious and hardworking Director for Africa, must have been very frustrated at times by my questioning. In spite of this, several good teaching projects were developed and in later years the more rapid effects of multi-drug therapy, MDT, answered many of my doubts. While it called for even greater regularity of supply, the treatment itself was for a much shorter period and more rapidly effective.

Life as Director was never boring. Even the routine was challenging. Decision-making is never easy – trying to find and keep a balance between the needs of the individual, the perceived good of the Mission, and effective and efficient management. Being a Christian community doesn't prevent problems from occurring and sometimes it complicates the solution. There were always lessons to be learned.

You rarely have all the facts you'd like to have in a given situation. Action has to be based on the information available, realising that it's incomplete, and on your own sensitivity. Guided, you hope and trust, by the Holy Spirit. Hard decisions postponed don't usually go away. Instead they become harder to make, and many decisions aren't between clear black and white but involve choosing the least grey.

While friends and colleagues are usually willing to offer opinion and advice, the point of decision is often a lonely place to be. However much people are drawn into discussion and consultation, at the moment of choice colleagues stand back. The decision and its consequences are yours alone. The fact that I worked happily as Director for 13 years suggests that I got at least 51 per cent of the decisions right. I hope.

Sky, sea, land, Watercolour, 1999

CHAPTER FOURTEEN
Mother Theresa

Mother Theresa was relatively unknown when we first met in the mid-1950s. She and I were invited to join an Indian State Government committee to coordinate and widen the area's leprosy work. She was a powerful character. Strong and stubborn, she was unshakeable in her convictions and opinions. I soon learned that there was little point in arguing with her and no chance of changing her mind. Even her humility was powerful. Working with her could be hard going but her compassion made up for the frustrations. There was a warmth about her that always came through any disagreements.

During this time Barbara was serving as a voluntary prison visitor in Purulia. She'd been invited to do it through her work on a government welfare committee whose main purpose was to encourage and accelerate 'village uplift' as it was then called. It aimed to encourage village development in deprived areas around Purulia with emphasis on the needs of women and children. They placed welfare workers and craft teachers in a number of villages to help increase family income, and improved the training and location of *dais*, village midwives. Most of these were experienced women who had the trust of the people but used traditional village practices which were not always very hygienic.

There was a large jail in Purulia town with about the same number of inmates as we had patients. Barbara teamed up with a Hindu lady from the town and they became regular visitors.

On one visit they found two 15-year-old girls, one Hindu, the other Muslim. They'd committed no crimes but had been in jail for two years. The police had found them wandering the streets and had taken them into protective custody for their own sakes. Indian streets are no safer for homeless girls than the streets of British towns. They'd lost their homes through their

Barbara with Mother Theresa, London, 1975

parents' second marriages and had nowhere to go. "What can you do for them?" asked the Jail Superintendent. He turned to Barbara. "Can't you find them a home? They shouldn't be here. Why don't you take them and make them Christians?" She took the challenge. "We don't *make* people Christian," she said, "but I'll do something." She had no idea what, but agreed to find a home for the Muslim girl if her companion could do something for the Hindu.

She contacted several orphanages and children's homes but none was willing to accept a teenage girl of almost marriageable age. The outlook wasn't encouraging. Finally Barbara wrote to Mother Theresa. The answer came by telegram. "Send her immediately." Arrangements were made and the girl went off with a police escort. Meeting Mother Theresa ten years later Barbara mentioned the incident. "I don't suppose you remember the girl," Barbara began. "Of course I do," she responded, "and she's happily married with a family of her own." She then made Barbara write her a letter – in Bengali.

Contact continued occasionally. When Purulia began regular training courses Mother Theresa asked if she could send some of her leprosy workers. First came a shoemaker. He was followed by two nuns. Ecumenical relations were less open then and the odd eyebrow was raised but we took them happily. We hoped that the new skills we offered them would improve the standard of their leprosy care which didn't always match the high level of compassion her workers showed. Her Missionaries of Charity still thought in terms of long-term shelter rather than positive outreach. There was little skilled medical oversight. It was perhaps a useful counterbalance to the emphasis most other workers were putting on village treatment and control, but medical care was becoming an increasingly complex discipline.

During the Mission's centenary celebrations in 1974 public meetings were held worldwide. Barbara and I attended several, including one in Calcutta. Mother Theresa, now well known, was among those invited. Towards the end of the inevitable speeches she left her seat and asked if she could speak. "I thank God for The Leprosy Mission and its workers," she said. "It was their inspiration and dedication that set the example and gave me the courage to begin my work with leprosy sufferers." I'm not so sure about that, sooner or later her heart would have taken them in, but it was good to know how she felt.

In my early days as International Director I had asked for a thorough reassessment of the Mission's 30 or so leprosy centres in India. One result was that we decided one centre in Bihar wasn't fulfilling a useful purpose and should be closed. What to do with the land and buildings? Sale on the open market was a poor option. We didn't believe a centre which had been used for decades by leprosy sufferers would attract many offers. The State Government would probably have accepted it as a gift but with no guarantee about its future use. I recommended that we offer it to Mother Theresa to be used as a home for the elderly. She accepted the gift.

She came to the Mission's International Office in London. She had a companion, who said nothing but carried her 'briefcase'. It was a hessian shopping bag with a few scraps of paper in it. She spoke to the staff on her usual theme, encouraging us to be 'doing something beautiful for God'. Her deeply-lined, blunt-featured face lit up from within and her sincerity shone through her heavily-accented English. She also spoke of the poverty of spirit she found so widespread in the west. She thought it much worse than the physical poverty which faced her every day in India. Then came a brief signing ceremony over coffee in my office transferring ownership of the centre. As I handed over the deeds they were placed immediately in the shopping bag. Then she leaned forward, fixed me with her eyes and asked sternly, "Now, what about running costs?" I said "No" equally firmly. She was never one to miss an opportunity.

If she'd gone into business instead of following her call to become a nun, she'd have become a millionaire. There was a steely quality, almost a ruthlessness about her sense of purpose. But it was always on behalf of the poor and neglected, never for herself.

Mother and
child
Monoprint
1965

CHAPTER FIFTEEN
Calcutta & Beyond

During the years we worked in Purulia I held onto a dream. Among the many patients we regularly had to turn away were some from Calcutta. The city once had a small leprosy hospital but it had been closed. The reasons were obscure but it meant that there were few facilities for leprosy sufferers in a city of many millions of people. The local Hospital for Tropical Diseases ran a clinic, but leprosy generally had a low priority; most hospitals were overcrowded and refused to admit those with leprosy. An Anglican Brotherhood, the Oxford Mission, ran two small clinics, the Premananda Leprosy Dispensaries, but they were struggling in spite of a TLM grant.

Some of the patients who came to Purulia from Calcutta were more fortunate than others. They were those with no obvious signs of the illness who managed the journey by train or bus. The less fortunate walked a painful two hundred miles, often begging on the way. The condition in which they arrived was sometimes indescribable. We always offered them temporary medical care but often it wasn't enough. I can still see the looks of despair on many faces when we said we had no room to take them in. They needed longer care than we could give. My dream was to have a leprosy hospital in Calcutta to help these people but it remained just that – a dream.

It's not always easy to identify who had an idea first. During the 1980s in discussion with Dr. Handel Thangaraj, the Mission's Director for Southern Asia, we realised that our work in India was overwhelmingly rural. This wasn't surprising. Most Indians lived in villages, and the history of fear and prejudice had dictated that leprosy centres should be located well away from the towns. But the big cities were rapidly getting bigger as people migrated there in search of work. Overcrowding was appalling, particularly in Calcutta, and overcrowding invites the spread of disease. We felt that something should be done in the country's urban areas.

We began by opening a number of clinics in Calcutta and beginning survey work in a small area of the slums. During a visit to this work Thangaraj and I went to see one of the Oxford Mission clinics. They hadn't the staff they needed and money was short. We talked about increasing our grant. Then very tentatively they asked if TLM would ever think of taking over the clinics. In my mind I saw the place as it was and as it could be – the site for a new hospital. I said yes immediately without looking at Thangaraj. Even the Oxford Mission staff were surprised by the speed of the decision. It would take a lot of work but it was the chance I'd been waiting for. The dream was becoming a reality.

The clinic fronted onto one of Calcutta's busiest ring roads. Battered and overcrowded buses looking as though they'd just survived a major tank battle fought their way around the trams. Heavily loaded trucks bounced over ever-deepening potholes and belched continuous smoke trails of pollution.

Private cars and the city's yellow and black Ambassador taxis bullied their way through impossibly narrow spaces, horns blaring. Hand-pulled rickshaws wove a crazy pattern through it all, and pedestrians jaywalked, risking their lives each minute and presumably placing their hope in reincarnation. A hospital here would certainly reach the people and the incessant traffic noise would remind patients that they were still part of the city.

Walking the pavements was hazardous. Missing paving stones threatened the careless. So did the muddy pools around the occasional standpipes where people bathed unselfconsciously in the dirty brown water coming direct from the River Hooghly. Cows stood around feeding on heaps of rotting garbage, the remains of green coconuts and crushed sugar cane left by itinerant vendors. And in any open space someone would erect a little shelter. A piece of crumpled plastic supported by bamboo canes, a flimsy protection from sun and monsoon rain.

The site was small for a future hospital. It was on an empty corner of a Christian cemetery. Later the hospital superintendent, Dr. Vijayakumar said, "We have quiet neighbours." It wasn't the ideal choice for a place of healing and wasn't always as quiet as 'cemetery' suggested. Almost every day it was taken over by gangs of enthusiastic boys playing cricket. Their wickets stretched down the lanes between the grave stones which often acted as mute fielders.

We sought planning permission for a four-storey, 30-bed hospital with all the support services it would need. There were months of consultations with architects and lawyers and frustrating interviews with government bureaucrats. We also had to respond to local opposition to our plans. It took two years to overcome all the obstacles but eventually the hospital was up and running. It was soon a centre of high quality medical and surgical care. One of my last acts before retiring in 1987 was to declare the hospital open, the only beds devoted to leprosy sufferers in the city. It was a great day. The dream fulfilled.

There are very few contrasts as extreme as those in Calcutta. It is the vibrant centre of Bengali culture for art, poetry, film, music and politics. It has an intellectual and sensitive middle class. It also has some of the worst slums in the country. As time went on the Calcutta hospital began to build on what had already been done and extended its work into the slums, organising clinics for thousands of patients.

Early clinics were just weekly roadside stops under the shade of a struggling tree, its leaves coated in red dust. As confidence grew, we were offered the occasional use of rooms in small youth centres organised by young men who were struggling desperately to make life a little better and improve their surroundings.

Statistics can mean almost anything but about 15 million people live in Calcutta, five million of them in slum areas. At least they have a roof of sorts overhead. Another million or so exist on the streets, surviving under sacking hung from railings or tree branches, cooking on the pavements, living, loving and dying in the city's humidity. Maybe a hundred thousand had leprosy. No one knew the real figure but the disease was common.

On a later visit I went out with a team of paramedical workers to see the work they were doing. It was an area in which they'd just begun house-to-house surveys. Knocking on doors, explaining their purpose, slowly gaining the confidence of the people to the point where they'd allow themselves to be examined for signs of illness. It was slow, hard work and demanded quite heroic commitment. They had that.

Leaving the car with its driver we walked down a narrow street, turned into a narrower lane and entered a six-foot-wide alley. A little light entered but never the sun. There was no breeze, no movement of air. The buildings were a mixture. Some were of unplastered red brick, held together with a mud mortar. Others of flattened and rusting five gallon kerosene drums nailed to rickety frames of wood salvaged from rubbish dumps. Gaps were filled with cardboard and sacking. Roofs too were varied. Some had clay pantiles, others boasted corrugated metal sheet. The poorer simply stretched tarpaulins, often patched with pieces of salvaged plastic sheeting. The unpaved paths were marked by ankle-turning depressions where rain had fallen from the roofs and pitted the earth. In the rainy season the ground turned to mud.

We ducked through a low wooden doorway and stood in a small courtyard about twenty feet square. *Charpoys* – string beds – leant vertically against the walls surrounded by piles of firewood. A woman was beating one of the beds with a stick to dislodge insect visitors. Festoons of clothing hung drying on strung lines. Through the middle of the yard ran, or rather didn't run, a stagnant open drain. There was no piped water, a standpipe and a stinking public lavatory 20 yards away were the only facilities. Sixteen families, about 64 people, lived in the tiny rooms that led off the courtyard. Only one man had a permanent job. A few more found casual work as day labourers.

They were inquisitive, a few sceptical, but courteous and cooperative. In the examinations that followed our workers found three people with marks that suggested very treatable early leprosy. They would need to be followed up sympathetically and as discreetly as conditions allowed. So the work went on day after day, unspectacular but life saving.

But my overwhelming impression of Calcutta is the commonplace courage and pride that is an integral part of the people even in the slums. Walk there early in the morning and you'll see young men and women emerging from these alleyways, well groomed, dressed in clean clothes and dignity as they go to work. Fighting for a better life, refusing to give in to the poverty that could so easily drag them down.

More recently Barbara and I revisited the hospital. We sat through an outpatient clinic, saw mothers bring sick children, husbands their wives. We watched the skill of the surgeon reconstructing a patient's hand. In the second operating room a woman ophthalmic surgeon was working on a man with cataracts in both eyes. Dedicated medical workers doing all they could to make life a little easier and to stem a little of the suffering – the tide of poverty that washes up each day.

Later TLM accepted a similar challenge in Delhi, India's capital city. This time the site was an open piece of land on the city outskirts in an area developing piecemeal. There were small *bustis*, huddles of slum housing, next to small factories being built on reclaimed fields. Our site was several feet below the level of the road and contained a very stagnant pond but we reckoned we could cope with that. After similar struggles, the Shahdara Hospital became a reality and a centre of hope.

Durbar Square, Kathmandu
Watercolour
1999

CHAPTER SIXTEEN

Widening the Vision

During my years in the International Office we became more aware of other organisations involved in work for leprosy sufferers. Some were secular, others Roman Catholic. Whatever their motivation, we welcomed their commitment. The need worldwide was so great there was room for all. TLM may have been the first and largest, but we were always happy when others joined in. There were several smaller societies in the UK, more in mainland Europe. Newberry Fox saw the need for us all to draw closer together. As a first move he invited the other British groups to set up a joint United Leprosy Aid Committee. It included the Roman Catholic St. Francis Leprosy Guild, the Order of Charity, the Order of Saint Lazarus and ourselves. Through it we began to publicise World Leprosy Day and organise exhibitions and joint services in St. Martin-in-the-Fields in London.

At the same time things were happening in other parts of Europe. Sometime in the 1950s a Frenchman, Raoul Follereau, created World Leprosy Day. His own confrontation with the suffering of leprosy patients in Africa had moved him deeply. He was determined to publicise the problem and challenge others to help. He was a theatrical figure, of medium height, well built and no longer young. He was flamboyant in a long cape, a wide-brimmed hat, a large and very floppy cravat. His appeals were emotional and powerful.

In 1966 a meeting was arranged in London. Eleven societies met together from France, Germany, Switzerland, Belgium and the UK. It was a disorganised affair. We had much to learn. Newberry Fox took the chair. He spoke only English. I supported him, speaking English, a few words of German and fluent Bengali. The latter might have impressed but was of absolutely no use. Follereau spoke only French. The Germans spoke German and some English. The Swiss understood all three. It wasn't easy but there was goodwill and we soon realised that we could do more together than we could do apart.

So began ELEP, the European Leprosy Association, with my signature as a founder member. We opened an office in France and began to meet twice a year over a weekend. We exchanged information about where and how we worked, shared details of our budgets and began to co-ordinate our activities. There were too many people needing help for us to waste our limited resources in competing or duplicating each others' work in a particular country.

ELEP grew into ILEP, the International Leprosy Federation, going fully international and welcoming new members from the Americas and Japan. Today 19 societies are involved. The sessions became more organised, with simultaneous translation for main sessions. This had amusing moments. I developed a reputation for 'English humour'. I never did find out what that was specifically but found that a joke could often defuse the tension of a disagreement. Humour could be a prolonged business in translation. Those who understood English well laughed immediately. The French speakers laughed next when the interpreter got to the punch line, and the Germans followed a couple of seconds later, not because they lacked a sense of humour but because the joke took longer to put into German.

Simultaneous translation had other advantages. To hear a translation you had to use earphones. Sometimes discussions could be long-winded and boring. I used to take a Sony Walkman™ with me and there were times when I was listening quietly through my headphones, not to the debate but to a recording of Beethoven or Mozart. You just had to keep the volume low.

Inevitably there were misunderstandings, not caused by Beethoven or Mozart. We each had different ways of working and different interests. Some were committed Roman Catholic groups. Others like ourselves were not. Some were secular and not particularly sympathetic to the idea of medical and social work among leprosy sufferers having a Christian motivation. Other groups too were essentially national groups, each raising support in a particular country. Some were unhappy with TLM's international nature – which had been its stance since its first years – and wanted to confine our fundraising to the United Kingdom. We argued for tolerance and freedom of choice for people to support whomever they wished.

We each had different visions for the future. We were happy and sincere in our efforts to cooperate and even to share in the funding of important joint projects but for some that wasn't enough. There were a few who dreamt of one supranational leprosy organisation, a sort of federal movement which would be monolithic throughout Europe and into which we'd all be absorbed. This was the point at which we as a Christian mission had to stand firm. It wasn't always easy or popular. We wanted maximum freedom with minimum restriction. Cooperation was good, coercion wasn't. At one stage I was elected President for two years, a demanding role given the tensions.

ILEP led to other interesting experiences. We were invited to Rome by Amici dei Raoul Follereau, the Italian society. From a simple invitation to attend a public celebration it escalated into a Sunday morning service in St Peter's led by Pope John Paul. St. Peter's was full, about 7,500 worshippers. I was invited to lead prayers during the service which I did with the Pope standing at my side. Whether that was to check my theology or not I never found out, but I wasn't taken off by the Inquisition. It was a moving experience. We stood under Bernini's great canopy with its twisted black marble columns under

Meeting Pope John Paul in Rome, 1986

Michelangelo's dome and I thought of the centuries of worship that had gone on, in and around the site, since the days when Saint Paul was taken to Rome.

After the service we were taken into the Vatican. We were led up a grand staircase, along carpeted corridors and into a reception room. We sat and waited while functionaries scurried about, busy as ants. Some of our Roman Catholic colleagues were overawed by the occasion and I felt how difficult it must be for anyone in the Pope's position to maintain a sense of humility. But when he came to greet us he was warm and friendly and human like the rest of us.

Venice, Pencil sketch, 2000

CHAPTER SEVENTEEN
The Miracle

The excitement of a lifetime in leprosy work has been in the changes. We've learnt more about the illness and its treatment in the last 20 years than in the 2,000 years before that. We could say that about many things of course, but in leprosy care we've seen miracle after miracle. Not the heart-stopping one-off individual miracle, but the discoveries made by dedicated workers in both laboratory and field. The picture of leprosy has been transformed totally and new life given to millions of sufferers.

When we first began work at Purulia in 1950 most centres were still called *leper asylums*. They were places of refuge, where the rejected and disabled could find a lifetime's shelter from a hostile world. Some had changed their name to *leprosy home* but the emphasis was still on long-term care. More forward-looking centres, including Purulia, had added hospital to the name, hoping that some patients would be able to go home again after treatment. But that could still mean several years in hospital. And although that was a great chunk out of anyone's life, it was still better than a life sentence.

Fear of leprosy was widespread and powerful. It was also two-way. Neighbours' dread of infection was deep and inherited and they rejected sufferers and drove them to the edge of society. Patients themselves feared the prejudice and isolation they and their families would meet. Many walked away rather than endure it. There was shame too. Leprosy was thought of as a punishment for sin, a sign of God's displeasure. The sick often concealed early signs of leprosy, denying its reality and hoping it would go away. It usually got worse. Sufferers withdrew into themselves, lonely and alienated. This was how many came to us, beaten and in despair.

Little was known for certain about how leprosy spread. Many thought it highly contagious, a conviction that contributed strongly to the widespread fear of the disease. Others believed it to be hereditary, or sexually transmitted, and a cause for shame. Yet other theories suggested that prolonged skin-to-skin contact, as between mother and baby, was an important way of passing on the infection. Today, as a result of more careful research, we believe the germs are simply passed on through coughing and sneezing but that most people develop sufficient resistance to fight the infection successfully without showing signs of the illness.

For a long time the only hope of cure was regular and painful injections of chaulmoogra oil which was produced from the fruit of the chaulmoogra tree. Chaulmoogra had a long history. It is mentioned in ancient Hindu scriptures as a cure for leprosy. Not as an injection of course but recommended to be eaten. We were never really sure how much good it did. Some patients with early leprosy improved on it. Their patches grew smaller but this didn't really prove the point as some leprosy is self healing and disappears without any sort of treatment.

But things were changing. We saw the first, fairly tentative introduction of a new medicine – dapsone. One of its great advantages was that it didn't need to be injected, although some patients wanted that to continue. An injection is more impressive than a small white tablet. Within a couple of years excitement grew. Patients looked better, their patches receded and began to disappear. The microscope showed that the germs, the *Mycobacterium leprae*, were dying and slowly disintegrating within the body. This new treatment was gradually winning a battle.

Cautiously doctors began to declare patients disease arrested. They hesitated to use the word cured. It was too early for that and too great a jump from the old assumptions of incurability. But there was great rejoicing as patients were presented with signed certificates saying they were of no danger to the community and could go home.

The euphoria didn't last long. The educated world outside began to ask about the difference between the two descriptions *cured* and *disease arrested,* and village communities stuck to tradition. Leprosy had always been incurable, they said, and it still was. Patients discharged with residual deformity bore the most prejudice. "How can you be healthy?" they were asked. "Look at your hands – your feet – your face." Cautious official recommendations reinforced the attitude. Patients who'd had the most severe form of the disease were strongly advised to keep taking tablets for life as a preventive measure. Again questions were asked. "How can you be better if you have to keep on taking medicine?"

Rejected even by their own families, although that was often through pressure from neighbours, patients began to come back pleading to be readmitted. The deep disappointment was tragic. It was hardest for patients but frustrating for workers too. Now we had a cure we wanted to get things moving faster, to open up places in the hospital for active, treatable patients and to spread the benefits as widely as we could. The continuing prejudice was hard to fight and sometimes discouraging.

This led to two developments. One was to face the challenge of deformity and disability. Paul Brand's inspired work in developing reconstructive surgery was a dramatic advance. With physiotherapy, often over several months, clawed and immobile hands were being given new flexibility. Intricate tendon transplants were giving strength and use back to hands which in the past could only have been held out to beg. Similar things were becoming possible with feet damaged by repeated injury through lack of feeling caused by the destruction of nerve endings. Operations gave new movements to paralysed eyelids, preventing blindness. Noses could be reconstructed too and, as techniques became more sophisticated and more surgeons were trained, enthusiasm grew and spread. It all helped patients back into their communities by removing or disguising the physical damage.

Then, Paul Brand turned his attention to the causes of this damage and how it could be prevented. Others helped. One was Dr. Robertson, 'Uncle Robbie' as we knew him. He worked with us in Purulia. He was a New Zealander and an orthopaedic surgeon, tall and slim, white-haired, and with a slight quaver in his voice. He'd retired a few years earlier because of a hand tremor but was willing to help in any way he could. He was asked to concentrate on feet and try to develop simple sandals and shoes which would protect patients' feet from accidental damage as they walked.

He impressed our patients. In Hindu culture working with leather in any form was something only for the low caste, especially shoemaking. Yet here was a surgeon and a foreigner willing to do it for the sake of others. He and Paul experimented with new and old materials. One day we gathered in Barbara's kitchen to use her small kerosene baking oven to try to melt crystals of a new plastic. It was a material that could be moulded when warm to the shape of a deformed foot. There was fire and smoke and ruined baking trays but it eventually worked. It wasn't exactly high technology but it led to better things. Even lower technology was pressed into use. The main material used for soling sandals was, and still is, old discarded motor car tyres. The rubber is tough, hard-wearing and cheap.

Uncle Robbie found sleep difficult in the hot weather. He had a bedroom in our bungalow and his bed had the usual mosquito net. It kept out the insects but it cut down any movement of air. One night he decided to sleep without the net to make the most of what little breeze there was. The mosquitoes took their opportunity and woke him with their buzzing. In the dark and half asleep he groped around his bedside table for a small jar of insect repellent he'd left there. He smeared it on his face and arms. The mosquitoes went away and Uncle Robbie slept. The next morning he appeared for breakfast streaked in blue. The jar he'd found was ink for his fountain pen. We never found any blue mosquitoes...

But however hard we tried, however promising the advances, we couldn't deal with all the patients who needed help. The hospital and its outpatient clinics didn't reach them. So began the second development, the shift to what were first called SET programmes – Survey, Education and Treatment schemes – and later known as Leprosy Control programmes. Whatever they were called centres began to organise small teams of paramedical workers to move into rural areas. Thorough house-to-house surveys found many new and old patients. Health education programmes were organised to combat the fear and prejudice which was still rife. Purulia organised one of the earliest SET programmes in India – although the way had been pioneered in parts of Africa – and was also one of the first to offer formal training for this work.

The leprosy germ was proving to be a formidable enemy. It fought back. Some patients began to relapse. They returned to us frightened and dispirited. They were a minority but it was worrying. The germ was developing resistance to the medicine. Among the millions of germs in a patient's body a few seemed to be immune to the treatment. These multiplied and leprosy reappeared. A contributory factor was irregular treatment. It was hard to keep up a regime of daily tablets for five years or longer but, if you didn't, some germs would survive. We realised that if this trend continued a time would come when dapsone didn't work at all.

A worldwide search began for alternative drugs. Some were tried and discarded. Then attention focused on a treatment in which dapsone was used together with one or two other medicines. This was the beginning of MDT, the multidrug therapy which is standard treatment today. It was the start of a greater revolution than any before. The result of the discovery has been another miracle. Governments and voluntary agencies are now working with a growing impetus and enthusiasm to find and treat more and more patients. Some scientists now believe that patients with very early leprosy can be treated with a single-dose medicine although it's too early to be confident about this. Certainly it has dramatically reduced the length of treatment to a few months.

Today many patients never see a hospital at all, never need to leave home. Treatment is widely available. Focused health education attacks the old prejudices which injured patients as much as the illness itself. Fears are lessened. The number of sufferers worldwide – 15 million some years ago – has now been reduced to less than two million and is still falling. That's the good news. The bad news is that, in spite of all that's being done, there are still 800,000 new patients appearing around the world every year – 600,000 of them in India – and there's no sign yet of this annual rate of new cases falling. Many people are still at risk of severe illness and disability.

Recently the World Health Organisation has been working towards 'the elimination of leprosy as a public health problem by the year 2000'. This is defined as less than one patient in a population of 10,000. A number of countries now claim to be able to achieve this but it is an oversimplification of the problem and could cause harm rather than good. To claim this sort of success will lead people to believe that leprosy is defeated when it isn't. Even if

every case were found and treated, there would still be a whole generation of ex-patients with handicaps who will need decades of care.

Another problem is that the remaining patients are the ones who are hardest to find. Patients who live in remote parts of less-developed countries, in mountains and tropical forests, or in the slums of large, third-world cities. It's good to be enthusiastic but not to be over-optimistic.

Today we're moving towards the integration of leprosy into general medical care. Patients are being treated in general and primary health centres like people with other diseases. Integration is two way. Often the leprosy hospital welcomes non-leprosy patients and treats their health problems whether they have tuberculosis or malaria or need surgery. Visit a TLM hospital today and you may see 25 people in the same ward all recovering from cataract operations performed by a TLM ophthalmic surgeon, leprosy patients lying next to otherwise healthy people. Sit in an outpatient clinic and you'll meet people who have a variety of skin diseases – not just leprosy. The traditional prejudice and fear broken down by shared need.

But for me the most important change isn't in the treatment itself but the change in patients' attitudes brought about by the treatment. Patients have a new dignity. Before, many had been ground down by suffering, their self-esteem shattered by repeated rejection. Restoring self-confidence is a vital part of care.

As I look back I try to imagine the conditions under which our early predecessors worked more than a hundred years ago. They had no cure and no knowledge of how leprosy spread. They believed it was highly infectious. Yet with a special kind of courage they responded to the need. It must have been hard to watch the progressive deterioration of those under their care, knowing that so little could be done. A daily heartbreak for sufferer and worker. Love could be shared, food and shelter offered – and the comfort of a faith that accepted sufferers just as they were and valued them for themselves.

But some things don't change over the years. When Wellesley Bailey founded the work that eventually became The Leprosy Mission he showed a wide acceptance of Christians of many persuasions. Long before cooperation across denominations became usual he offered his help and financial support to people of many different church groups. Perhaps being a layman helped him avoid polarised theological positions. All that mattered to him was that they held the seeds of Christian compassion for leprosy sufferers and were willing to help them. Today we take that for granted. Then it was remarkable and God blessed it.

Today he'd react with wonder and joy at the changed outlook. He'd thank God for the technology that's made such a difference to people's lives. But I think he would also ask us to continue to remember the individual and personal need. Something so easy to lose in the pressure of reaching out to so many.

Morning mist, Nepal
Watercolour, 1998

CHAPTER EIGHTEEN
China

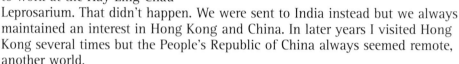

At our first interview with
TLM in 1950 we thought we
might be sent to Hong Kong
to work at the Hay Ling Chau
Leprosarium. That didn't happen. We were sent to India instead but we always
maintained an interest in Hong Kong and China. In later years I visited Hong
Kong several times but the People's Republic of China always seemed remote,
another world.

In 1981 Dr. Stanley Browne, TLM's Medical Consultant, was invited to visit
China. Several months later three Chinese doctors came to London. We invited
them to talks at the Mission. The leader was Dr. Ma Haide. He was a fascinating
man. Originally a Lebanese American, he'd gone to China in the 1930s as a
missionary. He was appalled at the misery he found, both medically and socially.
Disillusioned by the seeming impossibility of changing things, he left his mission
and joined Mao Tse-Tung and the Communists. He was with Mao on the whole
of the famous Long March. The Red Army was fighting Nationalist troops under
Chiang Kai-Shek and was defeated. It retreated into the north-west and in that
6,000 mile, two-year trek many thousands of Mao's followers died, some from
the fighting, many from disease and hunger. The rest regrouped, fought back and
eventually came to power.

Ma Heide survived both the Long March and the Cultural Revolution with the
terror and turmoil of its Red Guards. He went on to become a leading figure and
a legend in modern China. His name worked well for me later at the Chinese
Embassy in London. When eventually I was invited to China the officials in the
embassy were slow and cautious about granting a visa. I mentioned Ma Heide's
name and showed a letter from him. The visa was mine.

When he came to visit us in London he was the Leprosy Advisor to the
Government of the People's Republic of China. He and his colleagues asked for
our reaction should his government invite us to send in some short-term
teachers. They stressed that this was not an invitation yet. The Chinese didn't
work that way. To have risked an invitation being turned down might have
resulted in a loss of face, so it was important to know what our reaction would
be before an invitation was given. They were particularly interested in people
with experience in rehabilitation, physiotherapy and reconstructive surgery. We
said we'd respond positively and waited.

Little seemed to happen. Alan Waudby, who worked with me as Deputy
International Director, had spent years in Hong Kong and was experienced in
Chinese ways. He cautioned patience. He followed up the contact with a visit of
his own to China but it wasn't until 1985 that an official invitation came, not
yet to send in teachers but to share in the inauguration of the China Leprosy
Association and to take part in the first International Leprosy Symposium in

China in Guangzhou.

Barbara went with me. There were about 70 foreigners and 200 Chinese doctors, including Dr. Michael Waters who had succeeded Stanley Browne as TLM's Medical Consultant. It was an encouraging experience. The Chinese were open in discussion, there was a friendly atmosphere and a two-way willingness to learn. We had private talks with senior government officials but we were learning that, however senior the people with whom we spoke were, there were always higher officials behind them. And we had to wait for them to approve or modify what was agreed. But progress was made.

The city of Guangzhou was the old Canton, a bustling city on the Pearl River. It was full of energy, people and bicycles. I had an idea that the Chinese had discovered a way of breeding bicycles, there seemed to be far too many for a simple factory process. They were everywhere. The streets were dominated by them. There were trolleybuses, official taxis, but few cars. The bicycles had had their own revolution and had taken over. Men and women pedalled everywhere, most still in the grey or blue button-up tunics that characterised the revolution. Pedestrians were curious and friendly. The shops were well-stocked, building work was in progress everywhere. China was on the move.

After the end of the official programme Barbara and I stayed on with Paul and Margaret Brand to follow up some contacts made for us with local Chinese Christians. Laws governing religious worship were beginning to relax. We saw a mosque and an active Buddhist temple. Five churches had been allowed to reopen in the city. We visited two. One was a very active ex-Baptist church led by a team of three women pastors who were rejoicing over 65 baptisms during the year.

We attended the other on Sunday and joined morning worship. The church fronted onto a busy shopping street and, although it wasn't very warm, all the doors and windows were kept open. "We want people to see and hear what we do. There's nothing secret and if they hear, maybe they'll come in."

After the service we met a grey-haired woman in her 70s. A pre-Revolution university graduate, she'd also trained at the old Nanjing theological seminary as an evangelist. She was serene and joyful and still active, but she had suffered for her faith. She'd been arrested in the early days of the revolution for her Christian activities and had served eight years in jail. Released, she continued to witness as a Christian, was re-arrested and sentenced to a further seven years. At the end of our talk through an interpreter she suddenly said, "I have a Chinese friend in London. She's a doctor, a cancer specialist." She mentioned her name. It was the name of a friend of Barbara's. The Christian world sometimes seems very large. At that moment it seemed very small.

Alan Waudby followed up this visit a few months later and offered the services of the Mission's physiotherapy consultant, Jean Watson. She had worked in Hong Kong and was acceptable to the Chinese. She's been a tremendous part of the Mission, working at different times in Malaysia, the Northern Territories of Australia and Ethiopia and later making teaching journeys in many countries. Her visit was successful and was followed up by several more visits. It was the beginning of a very productive relationship with the Chinese that has seen a number of TLM workers offering their skills for the benefit of leprosy sufferers.

CHAPTER NINETEEN
Family Affairs

Behind every successful man, they say, is an astonished woman. That begs the question of what successful means. I think it's more a matter of relationships than external achievements or status. Barbara is the one who has encouraged me, provided most of the love, the uncommon sense and practicality families need. And cut me down to size in odd moments when delusions of grandeur have threatened. She is the extrovert in the partnership, the sociable one, the one always hospitable and welcoming to guests however inconvenient. She has a natural warmth which makes people feel at home and can find the practical advice folk need while I'm still analysing the problem.

She's a highly-skilled secretary and personal assistant. In the closing years of World War Two she volunteered for work with the Red Cross and had experience of nursing in local Nottingham hospitals.

During our years in India we worked together. She ran my office, kept me efficient and rooted my feet firmly on the ground. She took responsibility for the oversight of the 120 children under treatment in the centre and the slightly smaller number in the healthy children's home. This involved all their needs from clothing to education. She organised the children's Christmas presents. Father Christmas had been introduced years before although he came to Purulia on Boxing Day, presumably because he couldn't get everywhere in the first 24 hours. He was accepted with great enthusiasm.

She also organised the weaving department which kept two groups of patients busy. A number were weavers by trade and Barbara was often to be found in the noisy clack-clack of the hand-loom weaving sheds. They wove hospital sheets, bandage material, and *saris* and *dhotis* for the adult patients. We were never able to weave all the cloth we needed. A couple of times a year we had to buy much more on the open market.

Each time we needed about a mile of cloth. In the early days the cheaper varieties of cloth were rationed and we had to get permits to buy it from local government officers. Sometimes they were cooperative but not always. On one occasion I sat unsuccessfully with one official who refused to give a permit for such a large bulk buy. He was, he said, only authorised to give permits to individual people. I couldn't persuade him. Stronger methods were needed. "That's all right," I said, "I'll send my 700 leprosy patients down to sit outside your office and you can see them individually. When would you like them to come?" He changed his mind on the spot, I don't know why.

Cumbrian barn
Watercolour
1999

Our two daughters, Stephanie and Jennifer, were born in 1952 and 1954. The tradition among Europeans in India was to travel to Mission hospitals for the birth. The nearest one recommended to us was more than 400 miles away. It was a journey of three days, mostly by train. We couldn't see the point. Local women had children all the time without travelling that far.

Our own leprosy hospital didn't have the back-up facilities should there be complications. So against advice, raised eyebrows and murmured protests, we decided on an Indian hospital just 50 miles away. It was part of the great Tata conglomerate, a Parsi industrial enterprise that ran the country's largest steelworks and many other projects. It was in Jamshedpur, a two-hour drive away. The hospital had been set up for the benefit of the steelworkers and their families but was open to anyone.

The doctors and nurses were efficient and kind. Almost all the latter were Christian. At that time nursing wasn't seen as a good career for educated Hindu or Muslim women. Barbara was treated well and as the only European in the maternity ward each time, we're sure that we took away the right babies. Can folk in England say the same?

We were into Dr. Spock and his child-rearing advice in those days. We had a good *ayah* (a nursemaid) – Esther, from the local village but we differed at times in our methods. Esther, in Indian fashion, couldn't bear to hear a baby cry and would want to pick Stephanie up whatever the circumstances. One day, we'd fed her, changed her nappy and put her down to sleep in her pram on the veranda. The peace was disturbed by her crying. Esther rushed in. Well not exactly rushed in. Esther never rushed. Floated in gently is a better description. "Leave her, Esther," we said. "She'll go to sleep in a minute." The crying went on. Esther went to look. "You'd better come out here," she said, disapprovingly. We did. The pram had rolled off the veranda and tipped Stephanie out. She was lying with her head in the open rainwater drain. Fortunately it was dry. Esther said "I told you so" in Bengali. Spock hadn't allowed for that.

After Jenny, our second daughter, was born, she was lying in her pram out on the veranda one day when one of our staff carpenters came around. He was an elderly, grandfather sort of man, a little bent, a little gnarled, thin and grizzled. He considered the baby in silence. "Boy or girl?" he asked. Boys were important in local culture. "Another girl," we replied proudly. He shrugged.

Jenny and Stephanie, aged five and seven

"There's time yet," he responded and shuffled off. He was a good carpenter.

Barbara and I continued to work at the leprosy centre. The children grew up

healthy and were soon fluent in both Bengali and English. At Easter one year
Barbara told both children the story of Jesus' death and resurrection in English.
Ten minutes later she overheard Stephanie repeating the story to Esther in fluent
Bengali. She was five at the time.

Barbara organised their early education with the help of the PNEU – Parents
National Education Union – correspondence courses. This not only supplied the
material for teaching but compared children's achievements with others doing
the same course and gave a sort of benchmark for comparison. However, the
day for boarding school came all too quickly but Barbara made sure that both
the girls could read letters from us and write back before the separation came.

*Eddie and Squeak, Purulia,
c.1963*

We had great fun at home. We were into
pets as a family. I acquired two Rhesus
monkeys. One was a large mature male who
only stayed with us a couple of days. We
hoped he'd acclimatise but on his second
night he made a successful jail break. With
a colleague and a net from the hospital goal
posts, I spent a morning trying to catch him
but he loved our flat roofs and the drain
pipes were a delight to him. He'd watch
every move we made until we clambered up
our ladders and slowly approached him.
Then, when we were only yards away, he'd
casually unfold his limbs and leap
effortlessly into the nearest tree. He was fast
and far more athletic than we were. Our last
sighting of him was up a tree in the local
Christian cemetery. Then he disappeared.

The other monkey was small, young and
beautiful. An expressive pink face, round
liquid-brown eyes. We named him Squeak
because that's what he did. When not at large or sitting on my shoulder he lived
on the end of a very long light chain. It had a metal ring at the other end which
slid loosely up and down an eight-foot pole with a boxy house for him at the
top. It gave him freedom of movement and a place of safety from stray dogs.
Not that he needed it.

He befriended a neighbour's dog, a substantial and portly black mongrel
named Gagarin. The USSR had recently launched him into space. The original
cosmonaut Gagarin, not the dog. The two animals spent time together and
Squeak was often seen perched on Gagarin's back going for a ride.

Squeak was fascinated by the geese we kept. He found a weak link in his
chain, freed himself and went to investigate. There was a great honking and
hissing and Squeak appeared, a goose egg under his arm, making a mad dash
round the garden like a rugger three-quarter going for the line. The geese were
not amused but he was too fast for them.

Sometime later we were woken very early in the morning by distress calls and
a crashing in the trees. I got up. Squeak was not where he should have been. He
called. I looked around. He was about twenty feet up a tree at the end of the

garden, the loose end of his chain snagged inextricably on the spur of a branch. He was stuck. I began to climb the tree in my pyjamas. I moved out towards him, hanging with my arms and legs wrapped around the branch he was attached to. I got closer and tried with one hand to untangle the chain. He edged nearer muttering to himself. Finally he let go of the branch and sat on my head. He leaned forward until his face was upside down and within two inches of mine. "This is a fine mess you've got us into," I heard him say, although the family wouldn't believe it when I told them later.

The guinea pigs were prolific. They flourished in the warm climate and had a long netted run outside. We began with two and finished with 12. We gave two, a male and female, to the children at the leprosy hospital. They loved them. They named them *Dada* and *Boudi* – which means elder brother and elder brother's wife – their names for Barbara and me. That was fine until one day two grief-stricken children went in tears to Marian, one of our nursing sisters, to tell her that *Dada* had died. They meant the guinea pig although Marian didn't immediately realise it.

Keeping pets in India had its down side. We had two dogs – lovely dachshunds. With their low slung bodies they caused questions at times. "What are they? Dogs?" I heard a man say in Bengali as he leaned over our garden gate. "No," his companion answered, "they're rats."

One night there was a great commotion in the garden. Fritz, the larger dog had fought off a jackal. In the melee he was injured with a large gash down his shoulder. We bandaged him and he began to heal. Then his behaviour changed. He began to show worrying signs of serious illness. Fortunately the town had a vet. He took one look at the dog and asked to keep him for observation. Later he rang. It was rabies. He had to be put down and I had the difficult task of shooting our other dog. It hurt even more than the long course of anti-rabies injections we had to have to protect ourselves.

Putting the girls into boarding school in Darjeeling was tough and a great wrench for us. Barbara and I didn't feel we'd had children to be separated from them so soon and they looked very small and vulnerable as first Stephanie and later Jenny walked into the school. We felt just as vulnerable as they. Fortunately they both adjusted well and it was better than the traditional alternative of sending them home to the UK and not seeing them for several years. By going to school in India they were able to spend the three winter months of holiday with us in Purulia and either Barbara or both of us could get away for several weeks' holiday to be with them in the hot weather when we rented a cottage close by the school.

It was a long journey from Purulia to Darjeeling. First came ten hours by overnight train to Calcutta. Then a trek across Calcutta to the other main railway station and another train north. Halfway through the 20-hour trip we would detrain, gather coolies to carry the luggage, and stagger through several hundred yards of soft, shifting sand to cross the River Ganges by ferry boat. The river was a mile wide and there was no rail bridge across. Another struggle with sand and coolies on the far side and another overnight rail journey to Siliguri. Here there was a choice. Haggle for a breathtaking 60-mile taxi ride through the Himalayan foothills or take a final six hours on the narrow gauge railway that puffed sedately up the hills.

It was a Toy Town train, small but solid, and struggled slowly up the steep gradients. At some places two men would perch on a small platform on the front of the locomotive dribbling sand onto the track in front of the wheels to give better traction. Halfway through the journey at Ghoom the train would stop while passengers walked through the mountain mist to the station restaurant for tea, toast and omelettes spiced with chopped green chillies.

Later there was an airline, using old wartime DC3s – Dakotas. They were twin-engined workhorses, sturdy and reliable, and had been used widely to transport soldiers and supplies 'over the hump' into China or to drop paratroops wherever they were needed. The airline began as a combined passenger and freight operation. You sat on a seat running lengthways along the plane's fuselage, much as the paratroopers had, and your feet often rested on sacks of potatoes or crates of whisky. Landing could be interesting. The airfield was rough grass and was used most of the time by grazing cattle. The approaching plane circled the runway. Hearing it, a boy grabbed a bicycle and rode out with a stick in his hand to drive the animals out of the way. Once the area was clear the plane came into land.

Mount Hermon was a good school with fine teachers. There was a wonderful mix of children of about twenty nationalities. Most western European countries were represented and added to a wide spread of children from Asia, mostly India, Bhutan, Nepal and Thailand. There were some Tibetans too sponsored by the Dalai Lama who was then, as now, in exile in India.

The Christian atmosphere was positive but unpressurised. We'd considered other Christian schools in India but found them far too self-conscious and aggressive in their approach. There was a good musical programme and it was great fun to attend their shows. One highlight was Gilbert and Sullivan's *H.M.S. Pinafore* with a multinational cast of pupils lustily singing *For he is an Englishman*. The school was visited occasionally by groups of travelling actors. The best was a group on which the film *Shakespearewallah* was later based. It was a family group and among the family was Felicity Kendal, later to become famous in television's *The Good Life*.

During the time the children were in school Barbara grew closer to the community in Purulia town and made many Indian friends. She became a prison visitor, as I mentioned in Chapter 14, and part of a State Government Social Welfare Committee.

When China began its invasion of India in 1962 its troops penetrated the eastern Himalayas through Tibet. Darjeeling wasn't on its direct route but it was part of an area into which the conflict might spread. The school was evacuated. All civilian air flights were cancelled. The children were shepherded down the hills and onto trains for Calcutta, but the railway gave priority to troops heading north rather than to schoolchildren going south. We were among worried parents in Calcutta waiting for news. There was none. We spent three anxious days moving between the city's two railway stations meeting every train that came in. Eventually they arrived. They were dirty, tired and very hungry, but excited and safe. Their teacher escorts were even more tired.

On our return to England our resettlement in Ealing was traumatic for Barbara. In India we'd worked together and Barbara had a full and rewarding role. In London that all changed. The International Office had no position for wives. My work widened, offering more responsibility and travel for me but not for Barbara. With Stephanie at the local grammar school and Jenny at primary, Barbara was tied to the home as never before. She had lost all the variety and responsibility of her work in India. She had a lot to cope with. I was putting in full days at the Mission and taking off on four to six week journeys in Africa and Asia and away for three or four months each year. Family crises usually happened when I was several thousand miles away. Barbara was the focal point of stability who held the family together without complaint, sometimes at great cost to herself.

Adjustment wasn't easy for the children either. Making new friends meant breaking into already established groups in school. The English weather was often cold. There were restrictions unnecessary in India. We'd never had the slightest fear for their safety in an Indian environment. Coming to London changed all that. But with the resilience of youth they adapted.

The local church was some consolation, particularly for Barbara. It was lively, active and welcoming. We made many friends and immersed ourselves in its activities. She also joined the Meals on Wheels service of the WRVS and made friends there. As the children grew older Barbara found work locally in a variety of roles, at one time or another working for a local solicitor, the Pakistani High Commission and others.

Her real break came in 1973. Dr. Ron Goulding, a former minister of our church, was appointed Secretary of the European Baptist Federation. This coordinated the work of Baptist churches on both sides of a divided Europe and encouraged cooperation between churches in the west and those often-persecuted groups in the Socialist countries under Soviet domination. He asked Barbara to become his personal assistant. It was the beginning of a very happy and fruitful time for her.

Her work grew and in 1977 she was responsible for organising a European Baptist Congress in Brighton. I remember the day she told me. I offered to help in any way I could, thinking of my own experience in fixing conferences, usually for 50 to 100 people. "How many are you expecting?" I asked. "About 5,000", she replied. I was out of my league. In the end the attendance at one event topped 6,600 and nearly gave the fire department hysterics. They were responsible for safety and didn't like the overcrowding.

The Congress was a great success. Several thousand Baptist Christians came from all over Europe, from Moscow to Spain, and with representatives from the USA. Two of the most notable visitors were Donald Coggan, then Archbishop of Canterbury, and Cliff Richard. They came on different evenings, one to speak, the other to sing. The Archbishop arrived in a chauffeur-driven Morris Minor and walked almost unrecognised into the hall. Cliff Richard came in a chauffeur-driven white Rolls Royce. Both performed well but it was Cliff Richard who was received rapturously by the East Europeans. He'd sung recently in Moscow and encouraged Christians there by his witness.

Invitations had come to Barbara to visit the USSR and Poland. Our visit to Moscow in 1974 was inspiring. Flying from India at the end of a tour, immigration at Moscow airport seemed grim. The blank-faced officials inspecting

Barbara with Christian Leaders, Poland, 1979

and stamping our passports looked menacing. I felt uncomfortable until I realised they were simply showing faces which immigration officers all over the world show – boredom, nothing more. Prejudice feeds on itself.

The welcome was warm, particularly at the headquarters of the All Union of Evangelical Christians (Baptists), the cumbersome title bestowed on them by the authorities. They worked under great restriction but the few churches open were packed tight for every service. About a thousand people crammed in everywhere, standing four deep in the aisles and sitting up the steps to the speakers' platform. During services there was constant movement. It was a bit disconcerting until you realised that people who'd been sitting for some time were getting up and offering their seats to those standing, a practical bit of Christian behaviour. Services were long with a minimum of two, usually three, robust sermons. Barbara and I were asked to speak. I was told, "The authorities don't allow foreigners to preach but you can give a greeting – and if the greeting lasts for 20 minutes we shall be very happy."

I told them about TLM's work with leprosy sufferers. I didn't intend it but people were moved to tears, and afterwards one elderly lady came to me and said that she'd been a patient herself. Others, mostly large, bearded men, came and planted enthusiastic kisses on our cheeks. The singing was led by a large choir. It was superb. Some of the members came from the Bolshoi Opera chorus. It couldn't have been easy working there as Christians. The choir leader was a huge Ukrainian, a great bear of a man, tall and wide-chested. "How do you get them to sing as they do?" I asked. "It's not me," he said. "Each time they sing as though it may be the last time they'll be able to sing." In Moscow, then, that was always a possibility.

We attended a baptismal service. Again the church was packed. Bearded men, old women in headscarves, their gnarled faces full of experience and hardship. Younger folk, fresh and hopeful. There were 14 candidates for baptism, aged from 18 to 65. It was a courageous step to take. The State demanded that each person register the decision with the police and risk the persecution that might come. The church made demands too. No one was baptised unless they had undergone two years of instruction and had brought at least one other person to faith. It challenged us to examine our own commitment.

Red Square, Moscow

It reminded me too of another baptismal service I'd shared in, in an Asian country where it was actually illegal to change one's faith. People had served terms in jail for doing so. I'd been visiting a leprosy centre and was invited to attend. We walked through early morning mist and down a narrow valley for a couple of miles. The valley narrowed even more and became a gorge. We heard the water before we saw it, a little brook winding its way around the rocks. We crossed and recrossed the stream, stumbling occasionally over tussocks of rough grass. Then came a small waterfall and a rock pool.

The water was icy cold. Around it a group of 30 or 40 local believers were singing hymns as we arrived. They were led by a local pastor. He said a prayer and then stepped into the water followed by the new Christians, a man and his wife and a 20-year-old student. It was a joyful crowd, but there was also a realisation of what could follow if they'd been noticed or were informed on.

In Moscow and throughout the Soviet Union there was some friction between different Christian groups and deep hurt below the surface. The people we met were in the churches which had accepted government registration. They were criticised by groups in the West who thought of them as compromising their faith by any contact with the authorities. Some western Christians deepened the

Baptism, Moscow, 1974

divisions by supporting those who refused to register with the authorities and who bore even greater persecution, and criticising those who registered. We never shared that view. No one became a Christian in the USSR in those days unless they were totally committed. The disadvantages were too great. It was too easy to make judgements from the safety of a western armchair. Charity among Christians sometimes seemed in rather short supply.

We drove to Poland, travelling through the corridor the East Germans allowed for travel to Berlin and beyond in those pre-*glasnost* days. The border guards were slow and suspicious but impressed by my larger than usual passport. With so much travel and the need for so many visas and official stamps, mine ran to 96 pages. They couldn't understand how anyone would be allowed to travel so widely or so freely. Things speeded up though when they read my profession – Leprosy Advisor.

The Polish visit was memorable. We met and stayed with Christians in Cracow, Wroclaw and Warsaw. We visited the infamous Nazi extermination camp at Auschwitz, a deeply moving experience. There was the entrance, a great iron double gate with the words *Arbeit Macht Frei – Work Frees You* – above it and entwined in the handle a single red tulip. We stood and prayed at the wall where thousands of Jews and others had been shot before it was realised that the gas chambers and ovens would be more efficient. We saw the rooms piled high with belongings the prisoners had left behind. A room of suitcases, one of shoes and boots, another piled high with human hair, and the walls covered in photographs of individual victims. Their captors were frighteningly methodical.

We also had invitations to visit Christians in East Germany and Hungary. Eventually the European Baptist office moved to Hamburg and Barbara felt she'd rather stay with me than move there! She moved into the headquarters of the Baptist Union of Great Britain as Executive Assistant and continued to be responsible for relationships with Baptists throughout Europe until she took early retirement in 1985.

Our daughters finished their formal education and training. Stephanie took an Honours degree in Social Anthropology at Sussex University before training as a social worker. She is now a deputy director of social services. Jenny trained at St. Thomas' Hospital in London as a physiotherapist and, after some time working in a Combined Services Rehabilitation Centre, now has her own busy clinic practice. The next generation is growing too. Jenny and Peter have Sam and Jessamy, Stephanie and Howard have Claudia and Georgia.

My marriage to Barbara has been a true partnership. The sense of security and trust that love has created has provided the basis for all that we've done. It, or rather she, has provided the wisdom and understanding which has strengthened and nurtured our relationship. I am and will be eternally thankful.

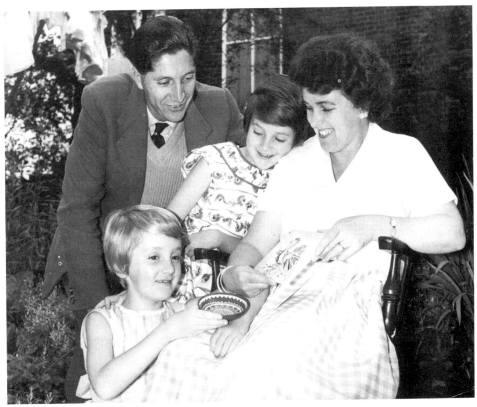

Eddie, Barbara, Stephanie and Jenny, home on leave from India, 1950s

Eddie and Barbara,
Nottingham, 2000

CHAPTER TWENTY

Pilgrimage

When Barbara and I were accepted by The Leprosy Mission we had no idea what the consequences would be. We'd grown up through World War Two and were used to making do and not having the comforts we now think essential. We had open minds and few preconceptions. We went to India blessedly free from prejudice – conscious prejudice anyway. But looking back I went with a young man's arrogance, believing I had something to give, to teach, to share. I quickly found much to share but it was India which shared it with me. I learnt much more than I taught, received far more than I gave. We learnt a lot, most of it pleasant and positive. At least, looking back it seems that way although there were difficult times. Separation from family and friends wasn't easy. Communication was slow and there were times when we felt isolated and a long way from home, but we slowly became part of the local community.

But in one sense I was playing a role. Attempting to be or to become what I imagined a missionary should be. Trying hard to live up to the apparent expectations of others. When I was baptised as a teenager the minister of my church gave me a text. It came from Paul's letter to the Philippians 4:13 *'I can do all things through Christ which strengthens me'*. The wording reads a little quaintly today but then we used the Authorised Version of the Bible.

It was a great promise. It helped take me through the years in the Royal Navy and college. I held onto it as we joined the Mission. But in the demands the work made on me the problem was that the promise didn't seem to work. I threw myself into my life in India with great enthusiasm. I enjoyed the learning, the language study and the adventure of a new culture, but as time went on I began to look a little more closely at the promise.

It wasn't true. I couldn't *do all things*. Why not? Because I had limits. I got tired. Other folk didn't always see a situation the way I saw it. I began to question the promise. If that wasn't true, what else wasn't true? One year on holiday with Barbara and the children in the cool and beauty of Darjeeling we went to the annual Christian Convention. Three days of Bible study and meetings usually with well-known speakers brought out expensively from the UK. They often had little understanding of the situation in India or of our needs and I didn't expect this speaker to do a lot for me. I have a low tolerance level for this sort of rather intense event but that year two things among the many things he said hit me with a clarity I'd never seen before.

First, there was a difference between what God wanted from me and what I wanted from myself. Read correctly the text *was* true. It promised that I could do all the things that God expected from me but not necessarily all the things I expected from myself. God doesn't ask the impossible. He knows that I can't go on indefinitely without a break and doesn't demand it. Only my own ego does that and ego can be hard to control.

Secondly, I grasped a truth I should have known all along, that God loves me as I am. Accepts me as I am. He respects personality. I don't have to play the roles forced onto me by other people, or even those I pretend to myself. It was a great moment of honesty, of facing the truth that God knows me as I am. There was no need for pretence because he could see through it anyway. It was a liberating moment. To be able to accept myself as I was and not worry too much about what other people thought of me.

It's so easy to turn the Christian faith into a straitjacket of control and limitation both for ourselves and for other people. That isn't what Jesus offers. His truth makes us free. But it can take courage to break the chains and step outside into that freedom.

I have a growing impatience with the 'rules' we Christians try to impose on each other. Christian formulae, creeds and self-conscious statements of faith leave me cold. I remember a friend in India, a monk who occasionally stayed with us in Purulia. His behaviour didn't always fit the conventional assumptions one makes about monks. For one thing he smoked evil-smelling cheroots – this in the days when we knew nothing of the damage to health nicotine causes. I questioned him about it. "I have enough trouble keeping the ten commandments," he said, "without creating any more." I may not have agreed with the smoking but I understood the point he was making.

Lifestyle is more important to me than the words we adhere to. It's the practical living out of love, imperfect though it may be in my life, that's important, not strict obsession with rules. Jesus made that pretty clear. I recently heard someone speak about *the need to break the tyranny of normality* – to refuse to do the expected or to accept patterns of behaviour pushed on to us by others. Jesus offers freedom. We have to find the courage to accept it and the responsibility that goes with it.

I began too, particularly in later years, to suspect that Christians who seemed to know all the answers probably weren't asking the right questions and that it was permissible to have doubts. I'm not comfortable with theological certainties or the dogmatism that goes with them. There are too many unknowns. Faith is a pilgrimage, an exploration into the continually new and expanding territory of the spirit. If ever I grab hold of a certainty and begin to feel comfortable about my faith somehow the Holy Spirit takes off, dances ahead and challenges me to think again. Invites me to step outside my complacency and continue the journey. I worry less about answers and even find myself willing to ask fewer questions. The excitement is in the travelling, in not knowing all the answers, in taking risks. In living with the uncertainties which is a truer test of faith.

One of my problems with God – he has many with me but that's another subject – is that he never tells me in advance what's going to happen. He never gives me a detailed map for my journey. He offers general directions but not itemised instructions for every hour of the day. It's more a sketch map with a general sense of whereabouts and a 'Here be unknown territory', rather than a minutely surveyed chart from the Ordnance Survey. And while I sometimes object to the lack of information it's better that way. I'm back to the freedom bit again. I simply have to accept that God is involved with each of us individually in a way I don't fully understand and get on with life.

It may be that God has a detailed plan for some people in which every little event is marked. I don't find it that way for me. The great thing is that he's in every situation with me and that his presence is dynamic. This offers an assurance that whatever each moment brings and whatever my next step will be, God will act within it. Starting from where I am. We need to remember that while he is a God for each of us he is also God of the cosmos, a loving mystery into whom we can only feel our way around the edges.

This brings richness and responsibility to every part of life. There are nice acceptable problems that resolve easily given a little thought, openness to others' ideas and some common sense. There are other problems we have to learn to live with, tensions that don't resolve easily, sometimes never do. And living creatively within these tensions is only possible with the strength that faith offers. That's sometimes easier to say than to accept and live out but it's the only way I know.

My experience of prayer has changed over the years. Like many Christians I used to batter God with my needs. Each morning I'd give him my instructions for the day. Tell him in some detail whom I'd like him to bless and strengthen, and what projects he ought to take a particular interest in. It was almost as though he depended on me for information rather than the other way round. I looked to him to change the world dramatically, especially the bit around me. I remember the story of a Muslim saint who said that as a young man he prayed for strength to change the world. As he grew older and little seemed to happen he prayed simply for strength to change his neighbours. Now in old age he said he just prays for the grace to change himself. That's where change begins, although at times I've been reluctant to accept it.

I've found that prayer needs fewer and fewer words. It's easy to crowd God out with too much speaking. Somehow we're not geared to listen, but prayer is a dialogue and the times of listening now seem more important to me than the words I say. Shortly after taking early retirement Barbara and I went on a three-day retreat. It was a great experience. Three days of silence. There were about 20 of us but no one trespassed on our time. We were together yet apart, apart yet together. There were no demands made on us. Not by the organisers anyway. The demands came through the silence. It was an opportunity to begin to clear out my personal storerooms, the attics and cellars, and to begin to look at all the baggage I was keeping and which I thought important. As I've continued the process of taking it out, dusting it down and examining it closely, I've begun to discard. The spaces created give a little more room in which God can work.

Silence itself can be prayer. It can also be self-indulgence, something that has to be guarded against. Long addresses to God don't seem to work as well as a less arrogant approach. In quiet God helps me search my mind and communicates in his way rather than mine. The silence of retreat, the opening of heart and mind to the God 'who is nearer to me than I am to myself' can be pain or joy. Pain when I'm shown things I don't want to know about. Times when he helps me dredge from the depths attitudes I didn't know I had. Joy in the quiet waiting without words and finding in it a presence hardly identifiable. And with it always a yearning for more. Waiting is the hardest thing. Since then I've been increasingly involved in the retreat movement, leading quiet days and longer retreats. I particularly enjoy prayer and painting retreats where we can use our creativity in quiet prayer.

I've drawn and painted ever since I can remember whenever the opportunity and the energy have coincided. It wasn't always easy in the heat and pressure in India but I was able to develop my painting in Darjeeling on holiday. I'd be up at dawn and out on the hillside among the pines with my watercolours struggling to catch the beauty of the changing light on the snows of Kanchenjunga and the other peaks. Painting could be interrupted momentarily by the sudden glide of a flying squirrel, all russet red and glinting in the sun. Going home for breakfast I'd throw stones on the tin roofs of neighbours' cottages to tell them it was a lovely morning and they ought to be out enjoying it. They didn't always agree.

Barbara and Eddie, looking at one of Eddie's oil paintings of Nepal

I held my first exhibitions there. The principal of the Bengali language school saw my paintings and suggested it. It was nothing grand, but it was successful in the number of paintings sold. Some folk envy 'the gift' for painting. It's true there has to be some innate talent to build on, however small, and its origin is mysterious, but it's not given fully developed. Gifts have to be refined by hard work and regular practice. Painting has no short cuts. In watercolour particularly one learns only by making mistakes. Again one needs to move out from the comfortable and the known into the discomfort and insecurity of the new and untried to explore and experiment. That's the only way to learn.

For me painting is the art of identifying the essence of a subject. Singling out the one thing above others that moves me in a landscape and responding to it in paint. It's the personal response that matters, not the detailed depiction of each little part. An artist is a brush not a camera. I can admire the attention to detail some painters give and the hours they spend working and reworking a particular passage but that's not for me. It's the spontaneity that counts, the attempt to catch beauty on the wing. To achieve the single brush stroke that holds the emotion.

A friend, Morgan Derham, once asked me as we were visiting a leprosy centre, "As an artist you're always looking for the beautiful and trying to capture it on paper. How do you cope with the suffering and daily ugliness of leprosy?" I was surprised. "What ugliness?" I asked. I'd not thought of it that way. By 'ugliness' I think he meant the misery and suffering untreated leprosy inflicts. This made and still makes me angry. It's something I rarely speak about but feel deeply. In the heat of a north Indian summer when energy drains away through the soles of your feet and tempers fray I was often angry with God. Not for causing the suffering but for allowing it. Angry with the communities which perpetuate it. Even angry with patients for not fighting and protesting more.

To stand in the room of a dressing clinic full of patients with stinking infected ulcers doesn't quickly reinforce a belief in the active love of God. But the work of the nurses serving them does. It can be difficult deciding where the pain comes from, but there's no doubt about the origin of the love that tries to deal with it.

Perhaps at the beginning of our life in India I had been repulsed by leprosy's carnage but not for long. One notices the disability medically and tries to assess it dispassionately. It's something to be taken into account in treatment or rehabilitation but patients quickly become individual people. Certainly leprosy injures bodies, causes great, sometimes calamitous, disability and handicap but one grows used to that. It becomes part of the norm and drops out of consciousness. Not that it's unimportant but one accepts it and looks to the person underneath. The proverb is wrong – beauty isn't skin deep. Ugliness is. Beauty often lies below.

Reaction to illness varies, particularly when it's something as serious and threatening to lifestyle as leprosy, but the human spirit can rise above it. Not just in fatalistic acceptance. One does see that, but there's often something more positive that can be seen, something that can transcend the tragedy, grab hold of life and wrestle it back. As we lived in India we gradually learned that there's a wholeness beyond physical health.

There's a healing of the spirit that can happen independently of the body. Patients can find faith both in God and in themselves. People who've faced the worst that life could give them, who've been disabled by disease and rejected by their communities can display an integrity I envy. Personalities which shine with an inner glow that lifts them above their suffering to a faith that is real, transparent and unquenchable.

We who work with leprosy sufferers are privileged to accompany them on their journey. Sometimes helping to make it a little smoother, a little more bearable. Helping them to find themselves, to re-grow personalities through the suffering. It doesn't always happen. Suffering can be destructive and some go down under the pain and alienation. There is an awful randomness in how leprosy strikes but an awesome triumph in the way some people fight their way through it. And as Christians there is something unique we can offer through our faith.

It has to be offered with care. Leprosy sufferers can be deeply vulnerable and what we have to offer has to be offered in humility. Aggression isn't part of the scene. Not everyone sees it that way. I remember visiting a leprosy hospital in Ethiopia run by a strongly evangelical mission to which The Leprosy Mission gave financial help. On the day of the outpatients' clinic there were many people at morning prayers in the church. I was impressed and remarked on it. "Yes," I was told. "We take the opportunity. We expect patients to come to prayers before they get their medical treatment." I found that hard to take. I told them that if they wanted continuing support from The Leprosy Mission that had to stop. Pressure has no place in the sharing of faith.

My books have given me another outlet for creativity. I've always enjoyed writing, from primary school compositions to grammar school essays, and editing the college magazine – my first real challenge. When I became the Mission's International Director I inherited the tradition of writing a monthly newsletter. It went out to workers around the world, many of them in situations where they needed encouragement as well as news. I began to include a '*God slot*' as journalists and broadcasters call it, a sort of thought for the day.

As time went on one or two people suggested they should be published as a book. I resisted the idea. Others made the same suggestion. Bill Edgar, the Mission's Communications Director, and I began to think about it. We put together some extracts but felt that something needed adding. I suggested the free-form prayers that have become such a part of the books. Some call them poems. I don't. There's imagery and imagination in them but I think true poetry is a high art form and I only play on the fringes. The manuscript then looked as though it needed lightening a bit. Bill suggested a few of my black and white line drawings. And so *A Silence and A Shouting* was born. The first of a series.

Since then there have been nine books and they've found a niche in the religious books market that no one could have foreseen. Certainly I didn't. With sales so far of more than 750,000 copies in all, they've brought a profit to the Mission of £1,750,000. I can't analyse why so many people have found them attractive and helpful. From my viewpoint the books have been an example of serving God more by accident than design, by staying open to his leading and creativity.

In my writing I try to be honest in what I say. "Well you would, wouldn't you. You're a Christian. Christian writing is honest." I'm not always too sure of that. There's some Christian writing around which doesn't seem all that open and is less than frank. It's not that writers set out to deceive, more that they write about an ideal rather than starting from where we actually are and which is easier to relate to.

It's not so much what's written as what's not written. There's a genre of

Christian writing which never admits to doubt or failure. It implies that if we are less than utterly successful in our spiritual journey we are somehow second class. If our illnesses aren't remedied immediately it's because our faith isn't strong enough. If our problems don't resolve rapidly it's because we haven't prayed enough. Reading that sort of book would leave me with an inferiority complex if I took it seriously. Fortunately I don't.

I write from where I am, admitting problems when I have them and being open to the weaknesses I share with the rest of humanity. Judging from the letters I get from readers this seems to touch a spot of great need for many and encourages them. Often my writing seems not to come from myself. Not that it's sent fully formed from elsewhere. There are times when I struggle for a day over one sentence; at other times the words flow. There's no telling in advance. One thing I have learned is that it's no good waiting for inspiration before you begin to write. Like painting, writing is a discipline that has to be practised almost every day. But there are times when I read an extract from one of my books quoted by another author or printed in a church magazine and I don't recognise it. "I wonder who wrote that?" I think, and then see the acknowledgement.

The other thing I try to do in my writing is to avoid jargon, the pious clichés which pepper so much Christian conversation. It's a kind of shorthand many of us understand but which sometimes sounds a bit precious to people on the fringe of faith. Better avoided.

Now in retirement I look back on a long and satisfying life with Barbara, the family and the Mission. We've lived through many deep joys, occasional disappointments, a share of both achievement and frustration. Not many people are blessed with a career that's given them great satisfaction and then in retirement find two more careers opening up in writing and painting. There's been drama and pressure. Travel in almost 60 countries. And through it all the feeling of being a tiny part in the purposes of God.

The poet Andrew Motion, whose poem I quote with permission at the beginning of this book, says the gift of daylight is temporary, its end inevitable. '*Darkness takes the edge of daylight*' he writes. It nibbles away at the edges of life and draws us in as we live on the edge between light and darkness. But it's the darkness that's temporary. We travel as pilgrims from the little light we have through the darkness into a greater light than we can imagine. That will be the last and greatest adventure of all as we are drawn into the splendour of the full light of God.

So far I have never been bored with life. I look to the future with great interest.

Deep winter
Watercolour
2000

Postcript

Tuesday, 30 November 1999. I was sitting in a hotel room in New Delhi trying to relax. It was early evening. I'd been in a conference all day and was tired. The phone rang. It was Barbara speaking from Nottingham. After a few words of family news she said, "I've got a brown envelope here from the Foreign and Commonwealth Office. There's another envelope inside marked Strictly Personal. What shall I do with it?"

Eddie preaching in New Delhi Cathedral during TLM's 125th Anniversay Celebrations in 1999

"Open it please," I answered. Barbara read it out. "Was I willing to allow my name to be submitted for appointment as an Officer of the Most Excellent Order of the British Empire?"

In other words an OBE. An honour for both Barbara and me, and The Leprosy Mission, and a recognition of work done. Even if literally there wasn't much of the British Empire left!

It was fitting that I should be in India when the news came through; the country where Barbara and I had first worked with the Mission, where we'd grown into whatever maturity we'd achieved, a country we loved, and where our family had grown up together. A country where we'd made a commitment that would last a lifetime.

This visit to New Delhi was as the Mission's Vice President to share in the meetings of its International General Council. Two days earlier I'd preached in New Delhi's Cathedral Church of the Redemption where we were celebrating the Mission's 125th Anniversary. I'd not been around for the whole 125 years, although it sometimes seemed like it, but by the end of November I was beginning my fiftieth year of association with it.

Almost six months later, on another Tuesday, 6 June 2000, Barbara and I, together with Stephanie and Jenny, went to Buckingham Palace to receive the award. We crossed the forecourt, passed the red-coated Guards in their black bearskin hats, entered the quadrangle and climbed the red-carpeted grand staircase. Life Guard sentries in plumed helmets, polished silver breastplates, white gloves and black leather thigh-high boots stood strategically on the stairs.

I was led with others into the Long Gallery where we had time to look at the paintings. Prominent were two famous Van Dyck portraits of King Charles I. In one he is on horseback, in the other he relaxes with his family. They seemed to serve as a wry reminder of human vulnerability that even touches royalty – Charles was beheaded in 1649 at the end of England's Civil War. I noticed no matching portrait of Oliver Cromwell, the Parliamentarian leader responsible for the King's execution! There were two Canalettos, sparkling in colour after cleaning, a Rubens and in the distance – yes, the gallery is that big – I thought I could identify a Rembrandt but at this point we were called to order.

We were briefed with great good humour on the morning's format, our names checked, and then we moved towards the Ballroom. It's a magnificent room and a great stage setting. Every last bit of plaster work ornamentation is covered in an exuberance of gold leaf. It must use a noticeable proportion of the country's gold reserves and some of it seems to have rubbed off onto the uniforms of the Palace officials! The room's high, decorated ceiling holds elegant chandeliers which drip light onto the players below, including Barbara and daughters sitting well placed in the front row, just a few yards from the Queen.

Her Majesty, backed by her Yeomen of the Guard in their 15th-century costume, two Gurkha Orderly Officers and her aides, stood on a dais and gently but firmly dominated the event. She was warm and friendly, and showed genuine interest in each of us as we were presented and given our insignia. She smiled, asked direct questions and chatted for a moment or two, and with a final handshake the investiture was over. The whole ceremony was conducted with a quiet efficiency and dignity and was refreshingly free of pomposity. Against expectation, it had been possible to relax and enjoy it all.

At the end we mixed with the crowd in the quadrangle, a rainbow sea of frilly hats and grey toppers in the sunshine. And finally, at the great wrought iron gates, a reunion with the rest of the family. Photographs and congratulations. A day to remember.

Looking at the award here on my desk it occurred to me that so many honours are designed in the form of a cross – the Victoria Cross, George Cross and so on. So is the OBE – a cross in gold with a pink ribbon edged in grey. I wonder why? The cross itself, at the centre of the Christian faith, is a symbol of service and sacrifice. Perhaps that's what the awards acknowledge. In our case the service has been tangible but the sacrifice is not something I recognise. Whatever sacrifice Barbara and I may have made over our years in The Leprosy Mission has been more than amply repaid by the joys of the work we've done, the experiences we've had and the friends we've made.

It seemed a great way to finish the story. In spite of the comment by the irate parent, mentioned in the first chaper of this book, we got a medal after all.

Barbara and Eddie, in the year of their Golden
Wedding Anniversary, with Jenny and Stephanie
after the Investiture at Buckingham Palace.

Stephanie, Howard, Georgia and Claudia, 2000

Jessamy, Jenny, Sam and Peter, 2000

LEPROSY MISSION
CONTACT ADDRESSES AND TELEPHONE NUMBERS

International Office
80 Windmill Road
Brentford
Middlesex TW8 0QH, UK
Phone: 0181 569 7292
Fax: 0181 569 7808
e-mail:friends@tlmint.org
www.leprosymission.org

TLM Trading Ltd. (for orders)
PO Box 212
Peterborough PE2 5GD
Phone: 01733 239252
Fax: 01733 239258
e-mail:
tlmtrading@dial.pipex.com

Africa Regional Office
PO Box HG 893
Highlands
Harare, Zimbabwe
Phone: 263 4 733709
Fax: 263 4 721166
e-mail: tlmaroju@icon.co.zw

Australia
PO Box 293
Box Hill
Victoria 3128
Phone: 61 39890 0577
Fax: 61 39890 0550
e-mail: tlmaust@
leprosymission.org.au

Belgium
PO Box 20
Vilvoorde 1800
Phone: 32 22519983
Fax: 32 22519983
email:olm03919@online.be

Canada
75 The Donway West,
Suite 1410
North York, Ontario M3C 2E9
Phone: 1 416 4413618
Fax: 1 416 4410203
e-mail:tlm@tlmcanada.org

Denmark
Skindergade 29 A, 1.,
DK - 1159 Copenhagen
Phone: 45 331 18642
Fax: 45 331 18645
e-mail:lepra@post3.tele.dk

*England & Wales, Channel
Islands and Isle of Man*
Goldhay Way, Orton Goldhay
Peterborough PE2 5GZ
Phone: 01733 370505
Fax: 01733 370960
e-mail:post@tlmew.org.uk

Finland
Hakolahdentie 32A4
00200 Helsinki
Phone: 358 9 692 3690
Fax: 358 9 692 4323
e-mail:
liisa.moilanen@kolumbus.fi

France
BP 186
63204 Riom Cedex
Phone/Fax: 33 473 387660

Germany
Küferstrasse 12
73728 Esslingen
Phone: 49 711 353 073
Fax: 49 711 350 8412
e-mail:LEPRA-Mission@
t-online.de

Hong Kong
GPO Box 380
Phone: 85 228056362
Fax: 85 228056397
e-mail: tlmhk@netvigator.com

Hungary
Alagi Ter 13
H-1151 Budapest

India Regional Office
CNI Bhavan
16 Pandit Pant Marg
Delhi 110 001
Phone: 91 11 371 6920
Fax: 91 11 371 0803
e-mail:
tlmindia@del2.vsnl.net.in

Italy
Via Rismondo 10A
05100 Terni
Phone: 39 7448 11218
e-mail:arpe@seinet.it

Netherlands
Postbus 902
7301 BD Apeldoorn
Phone: 31 55 3558535
Fax: 31 55 3554772
e-mail:
leprazending.nl@inter.nl.net

New Zealand
P O Box 10-227
Auckland
Phone: 64 9 630 2818
Fax: 64 9 630 0784
e-mail: tlmnz@clear.net.nz

Northern Ireland
Leprosy House
44 Ulsterville Avenue
Belfast BT9 7AQ
Phone: 01232 381937
Fax: 01232 381842
e-mail: 106125.167
@compuserve.com

Norway
PO Box 2347, Solli
Arbingst. 11
N 0201 Oslo
Phone: 47 2243 8110
Fax: 47 2243 8730
e-mail: bistandn@online.no

Portugal
Casa Adelina
Sítio do Poio
8500 Portimão
Phone: 351 82 471180
Fax: 351 82 471516
e-mail: coaa@mail.telepac.pt

Republic of Ireland
5 St James Terrace
Clonskeagh Road,
Dublin 6
Phone/Fax: 353 126 98804
e-mail: 106125.365
@compuserve.com

Scotland
89 Barnton Street
Stirling FK8 1HJ
Phone: 01786 449 266
Fax: 01786 449 766
e-mail:
lindatodd@compuserve.com

SEA Regional Office
6001 Beach Road
#08-06 Golden Mile Tower,
199589 Singapore
Phone: 65 294 0137
Fax: 65 294 7663
e-mail:
pdsamson@tlmsea.com.sg

Southern Africa
Private Bag X06
Lyndhurst 2106,
Johannesburg
Phone: 27 11 440 6323
Fax: 27 11 440 6324
e-mail:leprosy@infonet.co.za

Spain
Apartado de Correos, 51.332
CP 28080 Madrid
Phone: 34 91 594 5105
Fax: 34 91 594 5105
e-mail:
mundosolidari@mx3.
redestb.es

Sweden
Box 145, S-692 23 Kumla
Phone: 46 19 583790
Fax: 46 19 583741
e-mail:lepra@algonet.se

Switzerland
Chemin de Réchoz 3
CH-1027 Lonay/Vaud
Phone: 41 21 8015081
Fax: 41 21 8031948
e-mail:mecl@bluewin.ch

Zimbabwe
PO Box BE 200
Belvedere, Harare
Phone: 263 4 741817
e-mail:
tlmzim@tlmzim.icon.co.zw

ALM International
1 ALM Way
Greenville, S C 29601, USA
Phone: 1 864 271 7040
Fax: 1 864 271 7062
e-mail:amlep@leprosy.org

OTHER BOOKS BY EDDIE ASKEW

A SILENCE AND A SHOUTING

This is Eddie's first book of meditations and prayers. He says of prayer: 'Prayer is...resentment... irritation...impatience. Does that surprise you? It took me a long time to learn to bring resentments to the Lord, as well as my joys and requests.' Eddie takes one Bible text and talks to us about it, then gives us a prayer to use in our meditations.

DISGUISES OF LOVE

This second volume of meditations and prayers began, like the first, in monthly newsletters written for TLM's workers around the world. It follows the same successful format and is illustrated with his line drawings.

MANY VOICES ONE VOICE

Readers found encouragement, stimulation and challenge in the first two volumes of Eddie's meditations and prayers. This book is a further collection from monthly newsletters to Mission colleagues around the world. He dedicates it 'to many leprosy sufferers I have known, whose courage and faith have done more for me than anything I have done for them.'

NO STRANGE LAND

This volume was published in 1987 as he retired from the post of International Director. His humanity, integrity and artistry once more emerge in this collection of his chosen readings, thoughts and prayers.

FACING THE STORM

The fifth book in the series, once again shows Eddie's freshness, sensitivity and acute insight. The Bible references are drawn from Genesis to Revelations, each accompanied by a commentary and prayer and illustrated by his line drawings.

BREAKING THE RULES

The first book illustrated with Eddie's paintings in colour, this volume of meditations and prayers has a foreword by Wendy Craig, thanking him for helping to open her eyes and her mind, and enriching her whole experience of God's love.

CROSS PURPOSES

Focuses on six scenes from the Gospels where Jesus interacts with his friends and followers over a meal. With customary freshness and vitality, Eddie brings each scene alive, deepens our understanding of God's love and the purpose of Jesus's Cross to cancel out the cross purposes of the world.

SLOWER THAN BUTTERFLIES

Life is fast these days, and the demands of daily living press in, but in this book – a collection of passages written for 'Thought for the Day' for BBC Radio Nottingham – we are invited to step aside for a few moments and look at life around us, pause for thought and renew our perspective on the world. Each thought includes a suggested Bible reading.

MUSIC ON THE WIND

The latest book of his meditations and prayers takes us on an imaginative journey though the turbulent and earthy life of David the Shepherd and the King. David's story is one of a lifelong encounter with God through the good times and bad, and this can be our experience too as we open ourselves to the music of God's love. The book is beautifully illustrated with Eddie's drawings and paintings.

ORDER THESE BOOKS VIA THE ENCLOSED CARD OR THROUGH TLM TRADING LTD (details on page 142).